COLLECTIONS FOR YOUNG SCHOLARS™

VOLUME 3 BOOK 2

Country Life

City Wildlife

Storytelling

Art by Bonnie MacKain

COLLECTIONS FOR YOUNG SCHOLARS™

VOLUME 3 BOOK 2

PROGRAM AUTHORS
Carl Bereiter
Ann Brown
Marlene Scardamalia
Valerie Anderson
Joe Campione

CONSULTING AUTHORS
Michael Pressley
Iva Carruthers
Bill Pinkney

OPEN COURT PUBLISHING COMPANY
CHICAGO AND PERU, ILLINOIS

CHAIRMAN
M. Blouke Carus

PRESIDENT
André W. Carus

EDUCATION DIRECTOR
Carl Bereiter

CONCEPT
Barbara Conteh

EXECUTIVE EDITOR
Shirley Graudin

MANAGING EDITOR
Sheelagh McGurn

SENIOR PROJECT EDITOR
Theresa Kryst Fertig

ART DIRECTOR
John Grandits

VICE-PRESIDENT, PRODUCTION AND MANUFACTURING
Chris Vancalbergh

PERMISSIONS COORDINATOR
Diane Sikora

COVER ARTIST
Bonnie MacKain

Printed in the United States of America

ISBN 0-8126-3248-6

10 9 8 7

ACKNOWLEDGMENTS

Grateful acknowledgment is given to the following publishers and copyright owners for permission granted to reprint selections from their publications. All possible care has been taken to trace ownership and secure permission for each selection included.

Atheneum Publishers, an imprint of Macmillan Publishing Co.: *Cows in the Parlor: A Visit to a Dairy Farm* by Cynthia McFarland, copyright © 1990 by Cynthia McFarland. *A Story, A Story* by Gail Haley, copyright © 1970 by Gail Haley.

Bantam Books, a division of Bantam Doubleday Dell Publishing Group, Inc.: *Just Plain Fancy* by Patricia Polacco, copyright © 1990 by Patricia Polacco.

Christina Björk and Lena Anderson: "Linnea's Almanac: January" an excerpt from *Linnea's Almanac* by Christina Björk, illustrated by Lena Anderson, copyright © 1985 by Christina Björk and Lena Anderson.

Curtis Brown, Ltd.: *City Lots: Living Things in Vacant Spots* by Phyllis S. Busch, text copyright © 1970 by Phyllis S. Busch.

Children's Television Workshop: "City Critters: Wild Animals Live in Cities, Too" by Richard Chevat from the September 1988 issue of *3-2-1 Contact* magazine, copyright © 1988 Children's Television Workshop (New York, NY).

Clarion Books, an imprint of Houghton Mifflin Co.: *Aunt Flossie's Hats (and Crab Cakes Later)* by Elizabeth Fitzgerald Howard, illustrated by James Ransome, text copyright 1991 by Elizabeth Fitzgerald Howard, illustrations copyright © 1991 by James Ransome. *The Wall* by Eve Bunting, illustrated by Ronald Himler, text copyright © 1990 by Eve Bunting, illustrations copyright © 1990 by Ronald Himler.

Cobblestone Publishing, Inc.: "Growing Up Amish" by Joan Ennis fromthe June 1989 issue of *Faces* magazine: *Farm Children*, copyright © 1989 Cobblestone Publishing, Inc., 7 School St., Peterborough, NH 03458.

Crabtree Publishing Co., New York: "How Does the Garden Grow?" from *Early Farm Life* by Lise Gunby, copyright © 1983 Crabtree Publishing Co.

Dutton Children's Books, a division of Penguin Books USA Inc.: *The Boy Who Didn't Believe in Spring* by Lucille Clifton, illustrated by Brinton Turkle, text copyright © 1973 by Lucille Clifton, illustrations copyright © 1973 by Brinton Turkle.

Four Winds Press, a division of Macmillan, Inc.: *Sunflowers for Tina* by Anne Baldwin, illustrated by Ann Grifalconi, text copyright © 1970 by Anne Baldwin, illustrations copyright © 1970 by Ann Grifalconi.

Lydia Freeman: *Fly High, Fly Low* by Don Freeman, copyright © 1957 by Don Freeman.

HarperCollins Publishers: *Heartland* by Diane Siebert, illustrations by Wendell Minor (T. Y. Crowell), text copyright © 1989 by Diane Siebert, illustrations copyright © 1989 by Wendell Minor. "Filling the Ice-House" from *Farmer Boy* by Laura Ingalls Wilder, illustrated by Garth Williams, text copyright 1933 by Laura Ingalls Wilder, copyright © renewed 1961 by Roger L. MacBride, illustrations copyright 1953 by Garth Williams.

Holiday House, Inc.: "Carving the Pole" from *Totem Pole* by Diane Hoyt-Goldsmith, photographs by Lawrence Migdale, text copyright © 1990 by Diane Hoyt-Goldsmith, photographs copyright © 1990 by Lawrence Migdale.

Alfred A. Knopf, Inc.: "Aunt Sue's Stories" from *Selected Poems of Langston Hughes* by Langston Hughes, copyright 1926 by Alfred A. Knopf, Inc., and renewed 1954 by Langston Hughes.

Little, Brown and Co.: *Urban Roosts: Where Birds Nest in the City* by Barbara Bash, copyright © 1990 by Barbara Bash.

Lothrop, Lee & Shepard Books, a division of William Morrow & Co., Inc.: "Past" from *All the Colors of the Race* by Arnold Adoff, text copyright © 1982 by Arnold Adoff.

Gina Maccoby Literary Agency: "Raccoon" from *A Little Book of Little Beasts* by Mary Ann Hoberman, text copyright © 1973 by Mary Ann Hoberman.

Macmillan Publishing Co., a division of Macmillan, Inc.: *Home Place* by Crescent Dragonwagon, illustrated by Jerry Pinkney, text copyright © 1990 by Crescent Dragonwagon, illustrations copyright © 1990 by Jerry Pinkney.

Margaret K. McElderry Books, an imprint of Macmillan Publishing Co.: "Worlds I Know" from *Worlds I Know and Other Poems* by Myra Cohn Livingston, copyright © 1985 by Myra Cohn Livingston.

Morrow Junior Books, a division of William Morrow & Co., Inc.: *Johnny Appleseed* by Steven Kellogg, copyright © 1988 by Steven Kellogg.

Oberon Press: "The Worm" from *Collected Poems of Raymond Souster*.

continued on page 276

COUNTRY LIFE

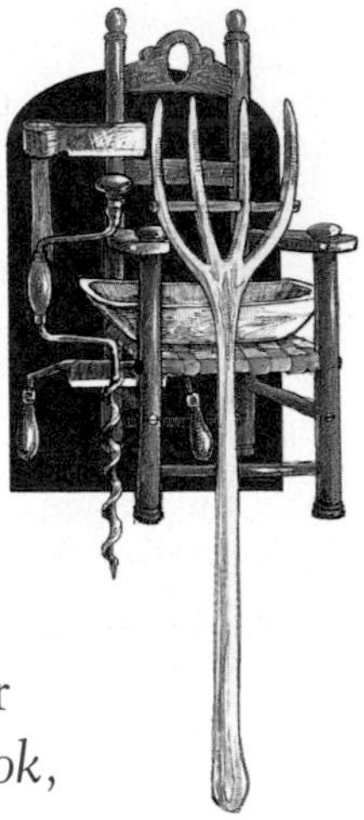

CITY WILDLIFE

STORYTELLING

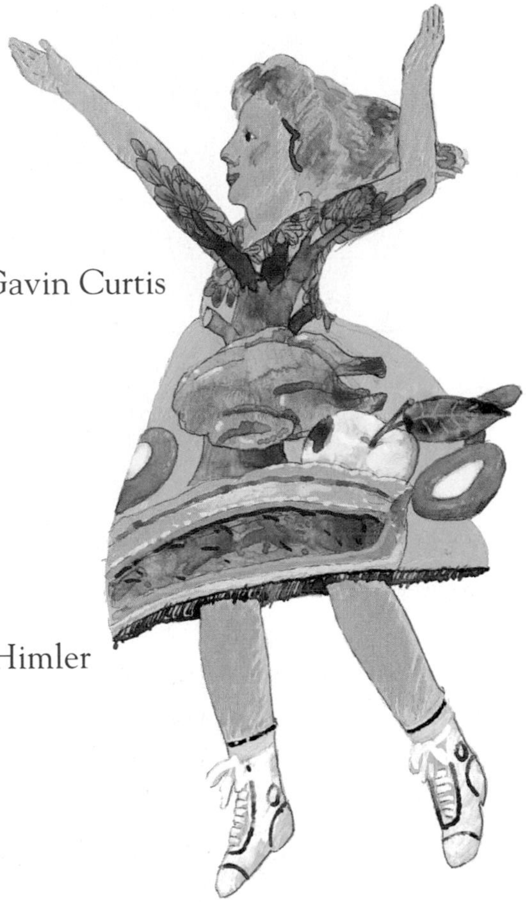

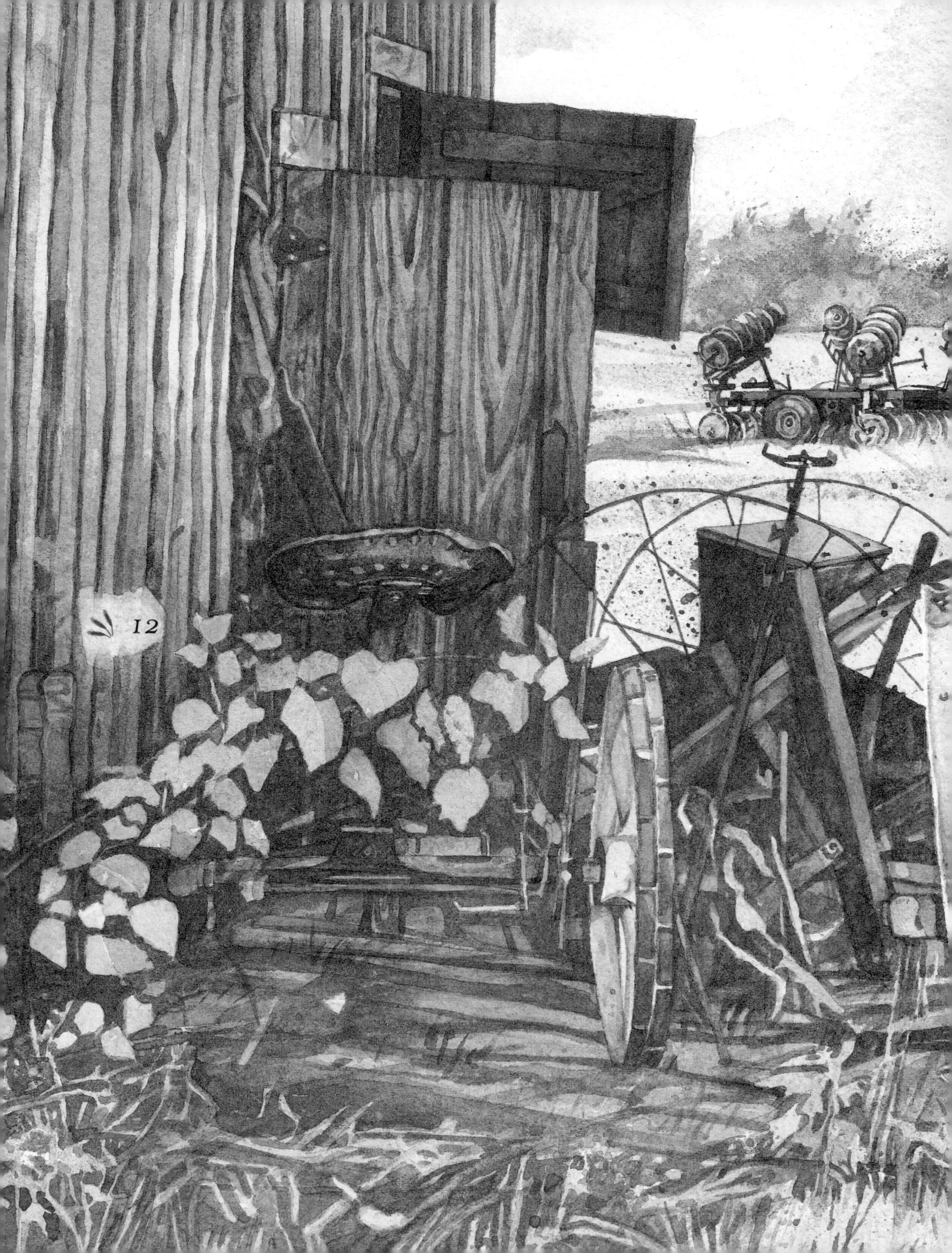

COUNTRY LIFE

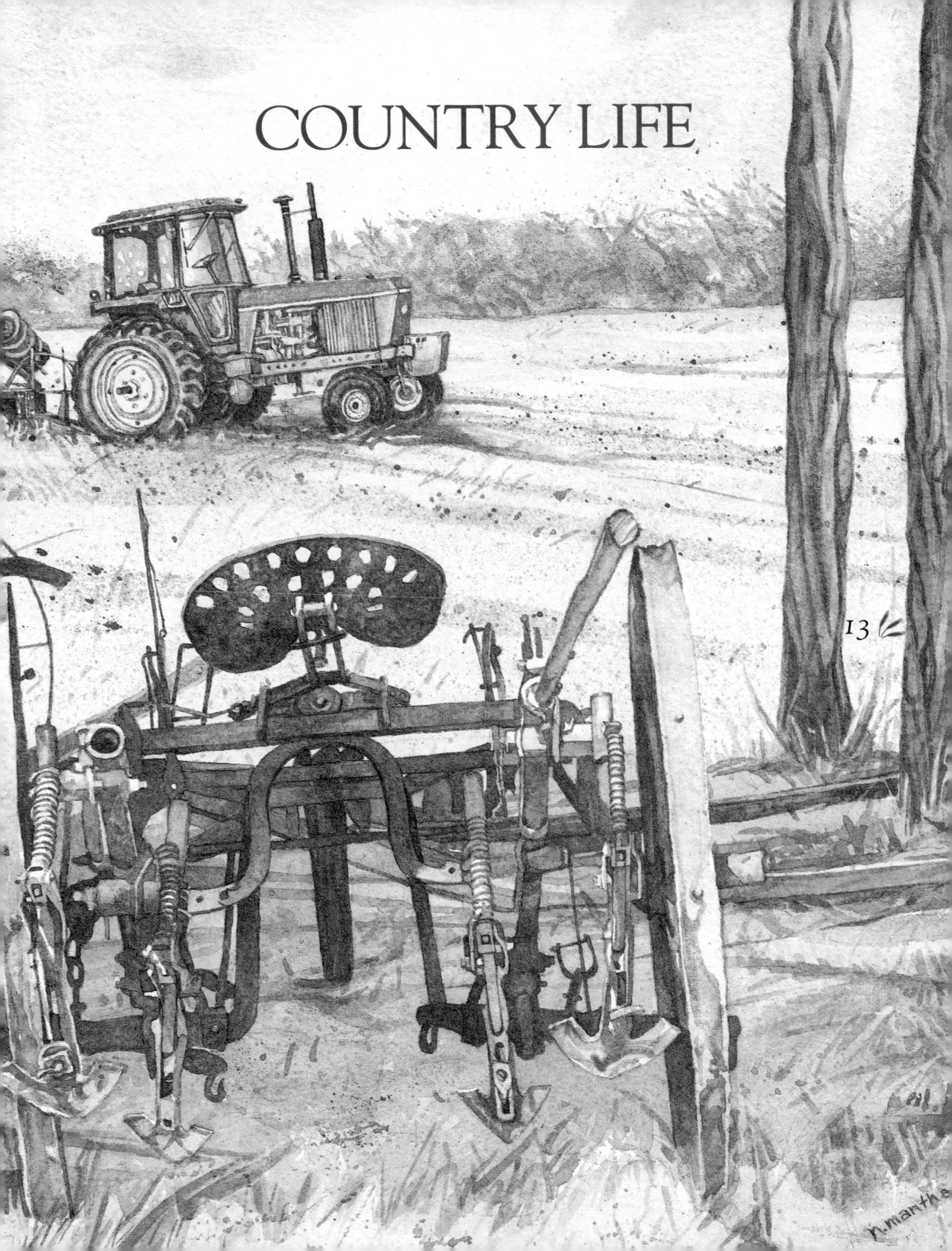

OX-CART MAN

Donald Hall

illustrated by Barbara Cooney

In October he backed his ox into his cart
and he and his family filled it up
with everything they made or grew all year long
that was left over.

He packed a bag of wool
he sheared from the sheep in April.

He packed a shawl his wife wove on a loom
from yarn spun at the spinning wheel
from sheep sheared in April.

He packed five pairs of mittens
his daughter knit
from yarn spun at the spinning wheel
from sheep sheared in April.

He packed candles the family made.

He packed linen made from flax they grew.

He packed shingles he split himself.

He packed birch brooms his son carved
with a borrowed kitchen knife.

He packed potatoes they dug from their garden
—but first he counted out potatoes enough to eat all winter
and potatoes for seed next spring.

He packed a barrel of apples

honey and honeycombs

turnips and cabbages

a wooden box of maple sugar
from the maples they tapped in March

when they boiled and boiled and boiled the sap away.

He packed a bag of goose feathers that his children collected
from the barnyard geese.

When his cart was full, he waved good-bye to his wife,
his daughter, and his son

and he walked at his ox's head ten days

over hills, through valleys, by streams

past farms and villages

until he came to Portsmouth
and Portsmouth Market.

He sold the bag of wool.

He sold the shawl his wife made.

He sold five pairs of mittens.

He sold candles and shingles.

He sold birch brooms.

He sold potatoes.

He sold apples.

He sold honey and honeycombs,
turnips and cabbages.

He sold maple sugar.

He sold a bag of goose feathers.

Then he sold the wooden box he carried the maple sugar in.

Then he sold the barrel he carried the apples in.

Then he sold the bag he carried the potatoes in.

Then he sold his ox cart.

Then he sold his ox, and kissed him good-bye on his nose.

Then he sold his ox's yoke and harness.

With his pockets full of coins, he walked through
Portsmouth Market.

He bought an iron kettle to hang over the fire at home,

and for his daughter he bought an embroidery needle
that came from a boat in the harbor
that had sailed all the way from England,

and for his son he bought a Barlow knife,
for carving birch brooms with

and for the whole family he bought two pounds
of wintergreen peppermint candies.

Then he walked home, with the needle and the knife
and the wintergreen peppermint candies tucked into the kettle,

and a stick over his shoulder, stuck through the kettle's handle,
and coins still in his pockets,

past farms and villages,
over hills, through valleys, by streams,

until he came to his farm,
and his son, his daughter, and his wife were waiting for him,

and his daughter took her needle and began stitching,

and his son took his Barlow knife and started whittling,

and they cooked dinner in their new kettle,

and afterward everyone ate a wintergreen peppermint candy,

and that night the ox-cart man sat in front of his fire
stitching a new harness
for the young ox in the barn

and he carved a new yoke

and sawed planks for a new cart

and split shingles all winter,

while his wife made flax into linen all winter,

and his daughter embroidered linen all winter,

and his son carved Indian brooms from birch all winter,

and everybody made candles,

and in March they tapped the sugar maple trees
and boiled the sap down,

and in April they sheared the sheep,
spun yarn,
and wove and knitted,

and in May they planted potatoes, turnips, and cabbages,

while apple blossoms bloomed and fell,

while bees woke up, starting to make new honey,

and geese squawked in the barnyard,

dropping feathers as soft as clouds.

MEET DONALD HALL, AUTHOR

Donald Hall first heard the story of the Ox-Cart Man from his older cousin in New Hampshire, who had heard it when he was a boy from an old man who said he had heard it during his childhood from an old man. It was always told as a true story. The story was first published as a poem in The New Yorker *magazine. Hall says, "When I was almost finished writing the poem, after about two years of working away at it, I had the notion that it might make a story for young children. It did."*

MEET BARBARA COONEY, ILLUSTRATOR

"I often go to great lengths to get authentic backgrounds for my illustrations. Ox-Cart Man *is the story of a New Hampshire farmer who lived in the last century. First of all, I had to establish* exactly *when the story could have happened. 'When' is very important to an illustrator because the sets (the landscape and architecture) must be accurate; so must the costumes, the props, the hairdos, everything.*

"To begin, I tackled the road that the Ox-Cart Man would have followed. This, I found out, would have been one of the early New Hampshire turnpikes, one which opened to traffic in 1803. This was a toll road. The Ox-Cart Man would have paid one and a half cents a mile for his two-wheeled cart.

"Next, I investigated Portsmouth and Portsmouth Market to ascertain what buildings would have been there between 1803 and 1847. The main difficulty here was that Portsmouth buildings, including the Market, had a bad habit of periodically burning down. It was a puzzle trying to figure out what was where and when.

"What finally determined the date was the Ox-Cart Man's beard. I wanted him to have a lovely red beard. . . . The story, therefore, had to happen between 1803 and 1847, when the turnpikes were busy, at a time when the brick market building in Portsmouth was standing, and when beards were in fashion. Thus, the date of 1832 was settled upon."

A REVOLUTION COMES TO THE COUNTRY

Karen E. Sapp

illustrated by Jan Adkins

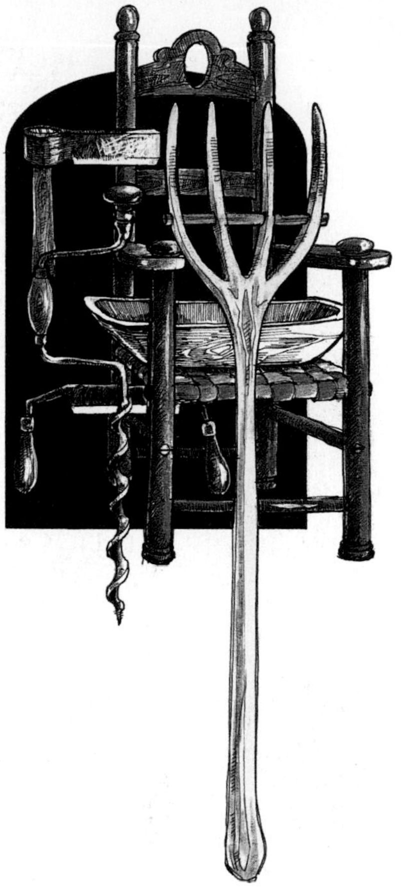

In the late 1700s, when the United States was still a very new nation, almost all Americans lived on farms or in small villages. Country life was hard and the workday was long. Farm families were nearly self-sufficient. This means they grew their own food and made almost all the clothing, furniture, and tools that they needed. Each member of the family played an important part in the family's survival. In the villages, craft workers such as tailors, cobblers, and jewelers worked in their own homes making items by hand, one at a time. Since most people produced little, they earned little. The few people who did live in cities depended on farmers and villagers for food and handcrafted goods. Cities were ports for shipping and centers of trade. They were not yet places where goods were made.

However, a movement that had begun across the ocean in England in the mid-1700s was just reaching the United States at this time. New inventions were beginning to change the way people worked and lived. This period in history became known as the Industrial Revolution. It is called a "revolution" because the changes that took place were great, and they seemed to happen suddenly. It is called an "industrial" revolution because the changes had to do with industry and manufacturing—the making of goods and products.

Before the revolution, manufacturing was done in people's homes either by hand or with simple hand-powered machines. For example, farmers used spinning wheels to produce thread, which was then woven into cloth on handlooms. With the invention of machines such as the spinning jenny and power loom, larger amounts of cloth could be produced more quickly by fewer people.

Many of these new machines were run by water power so they could not be installed in the homes of farmers. Instead

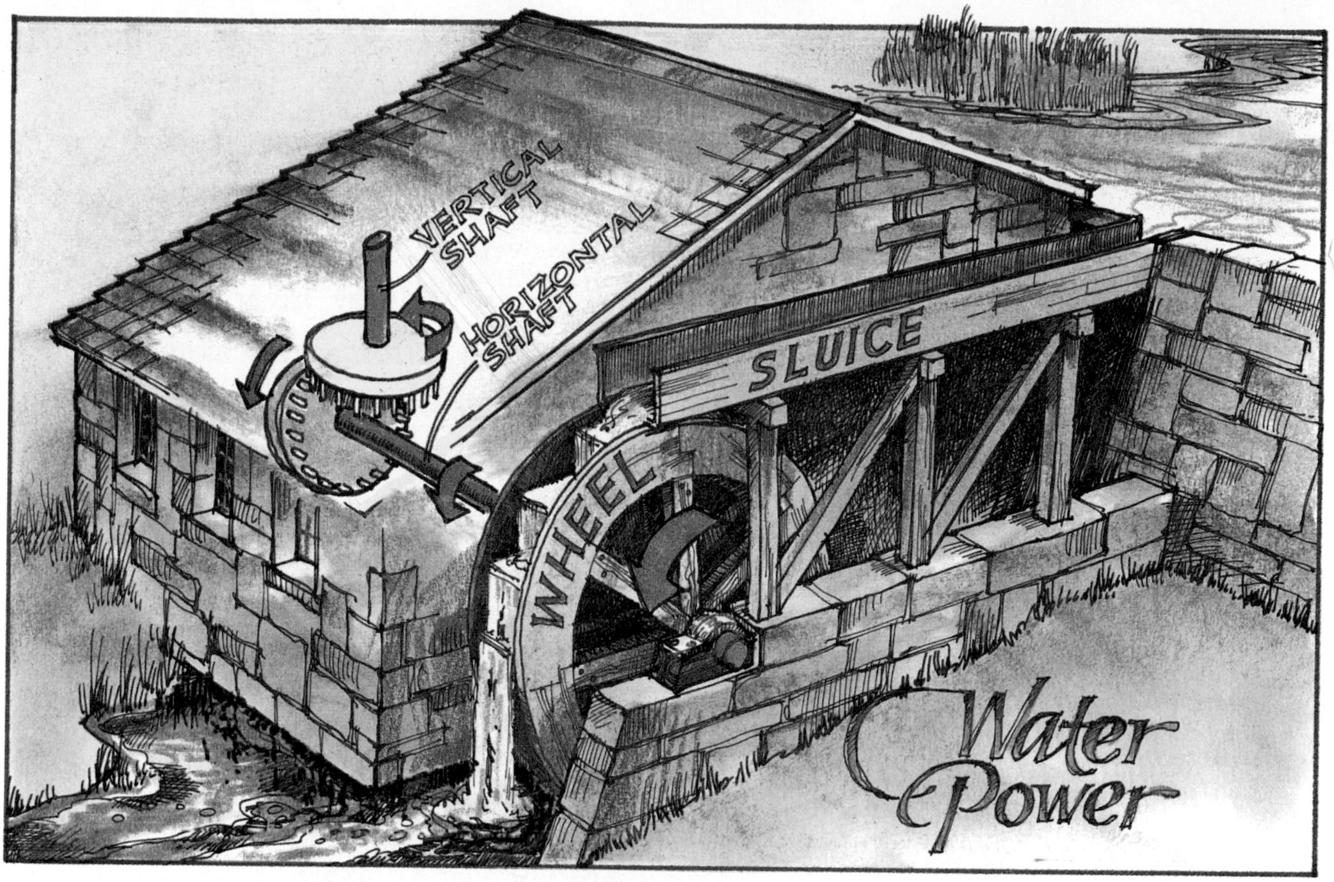

they had to be built near rivers or streams. For the first time many workers and many machines were brought together under the same roof in buildings called factories.

Machine-made products were less expensive and therefore more affordable. As more and more people could afford to buy factory-made goods, factories became larger and needed more workers. People flocked to the factories in search of jobs, and cities began to grow around these factories. Many people left their farms looking for work in the city.

Machines were changing almost every aspect of life in the United States. Factory owners needed more materials with which to manufacture their goods. They went to farmers for supplies such as wool, cotton, and food products. In order to keep up with the needs of the factories, people again looked to invention. Eli Whitney invented the cotton gin. It could clean as much cotton as fifty workers. The reaper, invented by Cyrus McCormick, allowed farmers to harvest grain much more quickly than before.

Many of the inventions of the Industrial Revolution required more power than horses or water wheels could provide. In 1785, James Watt improved the steam engine so that it could be used in factories. Large supplies of iron were needed to make these new machines, and coal was necessary to melt the iron. With the need for these supplies came better methods of transportation. Roads were improved. Canals were dug to connect the main rivers, and railroads were built to link American cities. Large amounts of supplies could now be transported more quickly from the country to the cities. In turn, factory-made products from the cities could be delivered to more people all across the country.

By 1916, only half of all Americans lived in rural areas. Many still earned their living by farming. They did their jobs so well, with the aid of the new farm machines, that they helped supply the whole world with food. But no longer did they have the time or the need to be self-sufficient. Farmers and city dwellers had become dependent on one another for the products they needed to survive. Today, more than three-fourths of all Americans live in cities or urban areas.

Life in the country has truly changed. Many people have left their farms and homes in the country for jobs and life in the city. City and country folk still need each other, however. Those who earn their living in the country supply the food and raw materials needed by people in the city. Those who live and work in cities and other manufacturing centers supply the finished products and machines that farmers need to clothe their families, furnish their homes, and run their farms. People in the United States today are no longer self-sufficient but have learned to work together to supply each other's needs.

HEARTLAND

Diane Siebert
illustrated by Wendell Minor

I am the Heartland,
Great and wide.
I sing of hope.
I sing of pride.

I am the land where wheat fields grow
In golden waves that ebb and flow;
Where cornfields stretched across the plain
Lie green between the country lanes.

I am the Heartland,
Shaped and lined
By rivers, great and small, that wind
Past farms, whose barns and silos stand
Like treasures in my fertile hand.

I am the Heartland.
I can feel
Machines of iron, tools of steel,
Creating farmlands, square by square—
A quilt of life I proudly wear:

A patchwork quilt laid gently down
In hues of yellow, green, and brown
As tractors, plows, and planters go
Across my fields and, row by row,
Prepare the earth and plant the seeds
That grow to meet a nation's needs.

A patchwork quilt whose seams are etched
By miles of wood and wire stretched
Around the barns and pastures where
The smell of livestock fills the air.
These are the farms where hogs are bred,
The farms where chicks are hatched and fed;
The farms where dairy cows are raised,
The farms where cattle herds are grazed;
The farms with horses, farms with sheep—
Upon myself, all these I keep.

I am the Heartland.
On this soil
Live those who through the seasons toil:

The farmer, with his spirit strong;
The farmer, working hard and long,
A feed-and-seed-store cap in place,
Pulled down to shield a weathered face—
A face whose every crease and line
Can tell a tale, and help define
A lifetime spent beneath the sun,
A life of work that's never done.

I am the Heartland.
On these plains
Rise elevators filled with grains.
They mark the towns where people walk
To see their neighbors, just to talk;
Where farmers go to get supplies
And sit a spell to analyze
The going price of corn and beans,
The rising cost of new machines;
Where steps are meant for shelling peas,
And kids build houses in the trees.

I am the Heartland.
In my song
Are cities beating, steady, strong,
With footsteps from a million feet
And sounds of traffic in the street;
Where giant mills and stockyards sprawl,
And neon-lighted shadows fall
From windowed walls of brick that rise
Toward the clouds, to scrape the skies;

Where highways meet and rails converge;
Where farm and city rhythms merge
To form a vital bond between
The concrete and the fields of green.

I am the Heartland:
Earth and sky
And changing seasons passing by.

I feel the touch of autumn's chill,
And as its colors brightly spill
Across the land, the growing ends,

And winter, white and cold, descends
With blizzards howling as they sweep
Across me, piling snowdrifts deep.
Then days grow longer, skies turn clear,
And all the gifts of spring appear—
The young are born, the seedlings sprout;

Before me, summer stretches out
With pastures draped in lush, green grass,
And as the days of growing pass,
I feel the joy when fields of grain
Are blessed by sunlight, warmth, and rain;

For I have learned of drought and hail,
Of floods and frosts and crops that fail,
And of tornadoes as they move
In frightening paths, again to prove
That in the Heartland, on these plains,
Despite Man's power, Nature reigns.

I am the Heartland.
Smell the fields,
The rich, dark earth, and all it yields;
The air before a coming storm,
A newborn calf, so damp and warm;
The dusty grain in barns that hold
The bales of hay, all green and gold.

I am the Heartland.
Hear me speak
In voices raised by those who seek
To live their lives upon the land,
To know and love and understand
The secrets of a living earth—
Its strengths, its weaknesses, its worth;
Who, Heartland born and Heartland bred
Possess the will to move ahead.

I am the Heartland.
I survive
To keep America, my home, alive.

FILLING THE ICE-HOUSE

from FARMER BOY by Laura Ingalls Wilder
illustrated by Garth Williams

The weather was so cold that the snow was like sand underfoot. A little water thrown into the air came down as tiny balls of ice. Even on the south side of the house at noon the snow did not soften. This was perfect weather for cutting ice, because when the blocks were lifted from the pond, no water would drip; it would instantly freeze.

The sun was rising, and all the eastern slopes of the snowdrifts were rosy in its light, when Almanzo snuggled under the fur robes between Father and Royal in the big bobsled, and they set out to the pond on Trout River.

The horses trotted briskly, shaking jingles from their bells. Their breaths steamed from their nostrils, and the bobsled's runners squeaked on the hard snow. The cold air crinkled inside Almanzo's tingling nose, but every minute the sun shone more brightly, striking tiny glitters of red and green light from the snow, and all through the woods there were sparkles of sharp white lights in icicles.

It was a mile to the pond in the woods, and once Father got out to put his hands over the horses' noses. Their breaths had frozen over their nostrils, making it hard for them to breathe. Father's hands melted the frost, and they went on briskly.

French Joe and Lazy John were waiting on the pond when the bobsled drove up. They were Frenchmen who lived in little log houses in the woods. They had no farms. They hunted and trapped and fished, they sang and joked and danced. When Father needed a hired man, they worked for him and he paid them with salt pork from the barrels down cellar.

They stood on the snowy pond, in their tall boots and plaid jackets and fur caps with fur ear-muffs, and the frost of their breaths was on their long mustaches. Each had an ax on his shoulder, and they carried cross-cut saws.

A cross-cut saw has a long, narrow blade, with wooden handles at the ends. Two men must pull it back and forth across the edge of whatever they want to saw in two. But they could not saw ice that way, because the ice was solid underfoot, like a floor. It had no edge to saw across.

When Father saw them he laughed and called out:

"You flipped that penny yet?"

Everybody laughed but Almanzo. He did not know the joke. So French Joe told him:

"Once two men were sent out to saw ice with a cross-cut saw. They had never sawed ice before. They looked at the ice and they looked at the saw, till at last Pat took a penny out of his pocket and he says, says he,

" 'Now Jamie, be fair. Heads or tails, who goes below?' "

Then Almanzo laughed, to think of anyone going down into the dark, cold water under the ice, to pull one end of the cross-cut saw. It was funny that there were people who didn't know how to saw ice.

He trudged with the others across the ice to the middle of the pond. A sharp wind blew there, driving wisps of snow before it. Above the deep water the ice was smooth and dark, swept almost bare of snow. Almanzo watched while Joe and John chopped a big, three-cornered hole in it. They lifted out the broken pieces of ice and carried them away, leaving the hole full of open water.

"She's about twenty inches thick," Lazy John said.

"Then saw the ice twenty inches," said Father.

Lazy John and French Joe knelt at the edge of the hole. They lowered their cross-cut saws into the water and began to saw. Nobody pulled the ends of the saws under water.

Side by side, they sawed two straight cracks through the ice, twenty inches apart, and twenty feet long. Then with the ax John broke the ice across, and a slab twenty inches wide, twenty inches thick, and twenty feet long rose a little and floated free.

With a pole John pushed the slab toward the three-cornered hole, and as the end was thrust out, crackling the thin ice freezing on the water, Joe sawed off twenty-inch lengths of it. Father picked up the cubes with the big iron ice-tongs, and loaded them on the bobsled.

Almanzo ran to the edge of the hole, watching the saw. Suddenly, right on the very edge, he slipped.

He felt himself falling headlong into the dark water. His hands couldn't catch hold of anything. He knew he would sink and be drawn under the solid ice. The swift current would pull him under the ice, where nobody could find him. He'd drown, held down by the ice in the dark.

French Joe grabbed him just in time. He heard a shout and felt a rough hand jerk him by one leg, he felt a terrific crash, and then he was lying on his stomach on the good, solid ice. He got up on his feet. Father was coming, running.

Father stood over him, big and terrible.

"You ought to have the worst whipping of your life," Father said.

"Yes, Father," Almanzo whispered. He knew it. He knew he should have been more careful. A boy nine years old is too big to do foolish things because he doesn't stop to think. Almanzo knew that, and felt ashamed. He shrank up small inside his clothes and his legs shivered.

"I won't thrash you this time," Father decided. "But see to it you stay away from that edge."

"Yes, Father," Almanzo whispered. He went away from the hole, and did not go near it again.

Father finished loading the bobsled. Then he spread the laprobes on top of the ice, and Almanzo rode on them with Father and Royal, back to the ice-house near the barns.

The ice-house was built of boards with wide cracks between. It was set high from the ground on wooden blocks, and looked like a big cage. Only the floor and the roof were solid. On the floor was a huge mound of sawdust, which Father had hauled from the lumber-mill.

With a shovel Father spread the sawdust three inches thick on the floor. On this he laid the cubes of ice, three inches apart. Then he drove back to the pond, and Almanzo went to work with Royal in the ice-house.

They filled every crack between the cubes with sawdust, and tamped it down tightly with sticks. Then they shoveled the whole mound of sawdust on top of the ice, in a corner, and where it had been they covered the floor with cubes of ice and packed them in sawdust. Then they covered it all with sawdust three inches thick.

They worked as fast as they could, but before they finished, Father came with another load of ice. He laid down another layer of ice cubes three inches apart, and drove away, leaving them to fill every crevice tightly with sawdust, and spread sawdust over the top, and shovel the rest of the mound of sawdust up again.

They worked so hard that the exercise kept them warm, but long before noon Almanzo was hungrier than wolves. He couldn't stop work long enough to run into the house for a doughnut. All of his middle was hollow, with a gnawing inside it.

He knelt on the ice, pushing sawdust into the cracks with his mittened hands, and pounding it down with a stick as fast as he could, and he asked Royal,

"What would you like best to eat?"

They talked about spareribs, and turkey with dressing, and baked beans, and crackling cornbread, and other good things. But Almanzo said that what he liked most in the world was fried apples'n'onions.

When, at last, they went in to dinner, there on the table was a big dish of them! Mother knew what he liked best, and she had cooked it for him.

Almanzo ate four large helpings of apples'n'onions fried together. He ate roast beef and brown gravy, and mashed potatoes and creamed carrots and boiled turnips, and countless slices of buttered bread with crab-apple jelly.

"It takes a great deal to feed a growing boy," Mother said. And she put a thick slice of birds'-nest pudding on his bare plate, and handed him the pitcher of sweetened cream speckled with nutmeg.

Almanzo poured the heavy cream over the apples nested in the fluffy crust. The syrupy brown juice curled up around the edges of the cream. Almanzo took up his spoon and ate every bit.

Then until chore-time he and Royal worked in the ice-house. All next day they worked, and all the next day. Just at dusk on the third day, Father helped them spread the last layer of sawdust over the topmost cubes of ice, in the peak of the ice-house roof. And that job was done.

Buried in sawdust, the blocks of ice would not melt in the hottest summer weather. One at a time they would be dug out, and Mother would make ice-cream and lemonade and cold egg-nog.

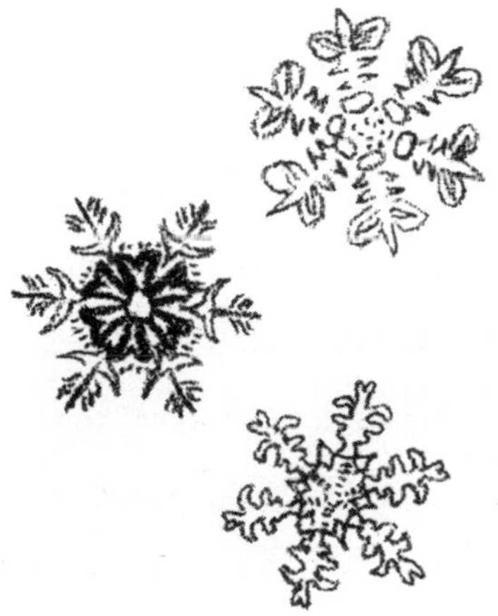

COWS IN THE PARLOR

A VISIT TO A DAIRY FARM

Cynthia McFarland

Every day is a busy day on Clear Creek Farm. Winter, spring, summer, and fall, the cows on the dairy farm must be milked—twice a day, every day.

When the snow is deep in the fields, and when the hot summer sun shines down on the pastures, the cows need to be milked. Even on holidays, Charlie Riddle, the farmer, must milk his cows. A dairy cow doesn't have a day off.

Maggie is a Jersey cow. Jerseys are always tan or brown. Some have white spots on their faces and bodies. They are friendly cows and like to be petted.

There are fifty cows on Clear Creek Farm, where Maggie lives. Fancy, Belle, Heather, and Sparkle are some of the other cows' names. It is not easy to think of names for fifty cows.

A tag with a number hangs from the chain around Maggie's neck. Another tag is attached to her ear. When a farmer has many cows, he needs a way to keep track of them. The numbers on the tags help him do this. The neck chains jingle and rattle when the cows walk or shake their heads.

When the wind is blowing and it is raining or snowing, the cows stay inside the barn. The straw makes a cozy bed when it is cold outside.

When the weather is nice, the cows like to graze in the pasture. The sunshine is warm on Maggie's back as she rests after eating. In the spring and summer when the nights are warmer, the cows sleep outside in the cool grass.

A cow doesn't have top teeth at the front of her mouth as a horse, a dog, or a person does. Maggie has a very long, rough tongue. By wrapping it around the tall grass she can pull off a bite and then chew the grass with her strong back teeth.

In the summer, Mr. Riddle and the farm workers cut grass, dry it in the sun, and make it into bales of hay. The cows will have hay to eat when the grass in the pasture is brown and dry in the winter.

But a cow needs more than grass and hay to make good milk. Charlie Riddle also makes feed from the corn that was planted in the spring. Machines chop the whole cornstalk into small pieces.

Then the silo is filled with this chopped corn, which is called silage. The silo is very tall. It can hold enough silage to feed the farmer's cows for many months. When snow covers the cornfields, there will still be food for the cows in the silo.

The cows eat their silage at a long trough, called a bunk. Mr. Riddle uses a tractor and feed wagon to take the silage from the silo to the bunk, where the cows are waiting to eat. The cows moo when they see the tractor because they know that soon they will be fed.

Maggie and the other cows know when it is time to be milked because Charlie Riddle and the farm workers milk them at the same time every day. If the cows are out in the field, they start walking up to the barn gate at milking time.

Early in the morning, when most people are asleep in their warm beds, the cows are being milked. In the evening, when most people sit down to eat dinner, the cows must be milked again. At Clear Creek Farm, the Riddle family eats supper earlier in the afternoon, or after the evening milking is finished.

The parlor in a dairy barn is not a pretty living room. It is the room where the cows are milked.

When Maggie comes into the parlor, her udder is firm and full of milk. She stands in a small pen, or stanchion, and the gates are closed so that she can't leave until she has been milked. Every time she is milked, her udder is cleaned and all the dirt is washed off.

Farmers used to milk their cows by hand into a bucket. That took a long time. Now there are automatic milking machines to make the job quicker and easier.

The milking machines don't hurt the cows. Suction from the machines gently pulls the milk from the cows.

The milk runs through shiny silver pipes into a large tank. There the milk is kept cold until it is picked up by the milk hauler.

When the hauler comes, he pumps all the milk into his long tanker truck and takes it to the creamery. There the milk is made into butter, cheese, ice cream, and yogurt. It is also put into cartons so people can pour a glass to drink or have some on their cereal for breakfast. In one day a single cow can give enough milk to fill more than fifty glasses.

To keep making milk, a cow must have a baby every year. Cats and dogs have several babies at a time. A cow usually has only one.

Maggie has just had a calf. The calf is sweet and brown, with large dark eyes like a deer's.

The calf nurses from her mother. That first milk is very important to the baby. It is rich with extra vitamins to keep the newborn calf from getting sick.

After the calf has been with her a day, Maggie will go back into the milking herd. Her calf will live with all the other babies. Each calf has her own small pen bedded with fresh, sweet-smelling straw. Mr. Riddle feeds them milk from a bottle, and they learn to eat grain from a bucket.

A calf is soft and warm and will suck on the farmer's finger, trying to find milk. She calls "maaa maaa" at feeding time.

Calves are frisky and like to play. After running and jumping, they take naps in the sunshine.

A female calf is called a heifer. A male calf is called a bull calf. Charlie Riddle keeps the heifer. Sometimes he sells the bull calves so another farmer can raise them.

Maggie's calf is a heifer. In two years she will be old enough to be bred and have a baby of her own. After she calves, she will be called a cow and will become part of the milking herd just like her mother, Maggie.

After the evening milking, Mr. Riddle finishes his chores. When the parlor is clean, the milking machines and pipes are washed, and the cows are fed, his day's work is done.

The cows finish eating their dinner and lie down to sleep. Soon bright stars glitter in the night sky above the quiet, dark pastures.

When the morning sun comes up again, another busy day will already have begun on Clear Creek Farm.

MEET CYNTHIA MCFARLAND,
AUTHOR AND PHOTOGRAPHER

Although Cynthia McFarland was raised in the desert of Arizona, she has since learned all about farming—from raising orphaned calves to driving a tractor. She lives on a farm in Ocala, Florida. "I truly enjoy my life in the country," she says, "and while I have no two-legged children, I have plenty of four-legged ones—horses, a pet sheep, numerous cats, and two dogs—to keep things happily active."

FINE ART
COUNTRY LIFE

Year 1860, Year 1940. 1949.
Grandma Moses.

Oil on pressed wood, 66 x 53.3 cm.

52

Husking Bee, Island of Nantucket. 1876.
Eastman Johnson.

Oil on canvas, 27 1/4" x 54 3/16". Mr. and Mrs. Potter Palmer Collection, Art Institute of Chicago. 1922.444.

Country Store, Alabama. 1936. Walker Evans.

Silver gelatin print. Library of Congress. Photo: PHOTRI

Sugar Cane. 1943. Thomas Hart Benton.

Oil and tempera on canvas mounted on panel. Lyman Field and United Missouri Bank.

GROWING UP AMISH

Joan Ennis

On a warm summer evening, teen-agers gather at a farm for a cornhusking party. Excitement fills the air. Boys dressed in long black pants with suspenders, dark shirts, and straw hats choose girl partners to husk corn. Girls wear long, solid-color dresses covered with an apron and shawl and bonnets over their white prayer caps. Everyone is barefoot in the warm, dry weather. After several hours of husking, talking, and laughing, the young people eat a hearty late supper and gather in the barn for games and square-dancing.

These children are Amish. Of the Amish communities that exist in twenty-eight states, most are in the Midwest.

©Jerry Irwin

Amish people first settled in Pennsylvania more than two hundred fifty years ago after emigrating from Europe to escape persecution for their religious beliefs.

All Amish children grow up in farming communities. Their church rules require people to be farmers or to work at farm-related occupations, and they believe that working the land keeps them closer to God. An Amish family grows, butchers, cans, or bakes most of its own food. The Amish reject electricity, cars, telephones, and the like as too worldly, things that take people away from the simple life. They work with simple, old-fashioned equipment.

Amish children learn obedience as toddlers when they sit through four-hour preaching services. By age four, they help their parents with chores. Family members work together on the farm, and the children have a sense of security knowing that they will grow up to be like their parents. Church rules forbid different behavior. Amish people believe that there is always work to do and that idleness leads to wrongdoing. The children do not know the risks and poverty that can exist on other farms because the community helps families in need.

In a typical family, everyone rises at 5:00 A.M. School-age children do their chores before walking to the Amish school. They divide up farm chores such as milking the cows, feeding and bedding the horses, hogs, and calves, feeding the hens, and gathering eggs. Young children bring wood into the kitchen. Helping on the farm becomes a way of life.

©Jerry Irwin

During the crop planting and harvest seasons, all family members help in the fields. After the harvest, children help husk corn. Those too young to help play nearby, running down corn rows and across pastures.

The children learn to garden at a young age, helping their mothers plant and gather the family vegetables. Girls learn to can and dry fruits and vegetables. Often by age ten they can bake bread and *schnitzel* (dried-apple pies shaped like a half-moon).

In contrast to other American farm children, Amish children attend a one-room Amish school through eighth grade. The adults believe that no further education is necessary for their way of life. At home, the children speak Pennsylvania Dutch, a dialect based on the German their forebears brought from Europe. ("Dutch" refers to *Deutsch*, meaning German, not to Holland.) They learn English at school in order to communicate and trade with English-speaking people on the outside. Arithmetic is considered important for farm economics and selling crops. As in the home, the children share chores at school, such as bringing in wood, cleaning the blackboard, and sweeping the floor.

©Jerry Irwin

After eighth grade when they leave school, Amish children work on the family farm or one nearby. Girls help in the home. Boys not needed on the farm may find a farm-related job, such as blacksmith, carriage builder, harness maker, or butcher. Some young people work in feed mills, sawmills, dairies, or cheese factories, saving their earnings for the time when they will marry.

Social gatherings center on farm activities, like the cornhusking party. Young people also gather for Sunday evening barn singing after a Sunday service and meal at a church member's home. The barn floor is swept clean, and lanterns are hung for the young unmarried people aged sixteen or older, who sing and square-dance until late in the evening.

Barn raisings create a joyous, holiday atmosphere. Perhaps a newly married couple needs a barn or a church member's barn has burned down. The entire community gathers to help build the new barn. The children look

forward to playing with friends while the men hammer. The children's laughter mixes with the talking, singing, and joking of the men. Occasionally they pause to watch the hammering and cutting and look up at their fathers and older brothers high on the frame.

Around noon, appetizing aromas waft through the air. The children hurry to the outside tables and benches to eat the hearty meal that the women have prepared. After lunch, the younger children run around and under a large quilting frame where girls sit with their mothers and practice their quilting stitches. Late in the afternoon, the barn nearly finished, the families return home to do their own chores.

The Amish live in a world valuing simplicity, family, and God. They wear different clothes and reject many things common in American society because they believe that their simple life keeps the family together and brings them closer to God.

©Jerry Irwin

JUST PLAIN FANCY

Patricia Polacco

Kaleb and his two daughters hurried along Lancaster County Road in their buggy. Cars whizzed by them, but they paid no mind. *Clop, clop, clop* went the horse's hooves on the pavement.

"Papa," Naomi asked, "why don't we have a car like the English?"

"It is not our way, child. We are in no hurry," he said as he drew up the reins and slowly directed the horse into their farmyard.

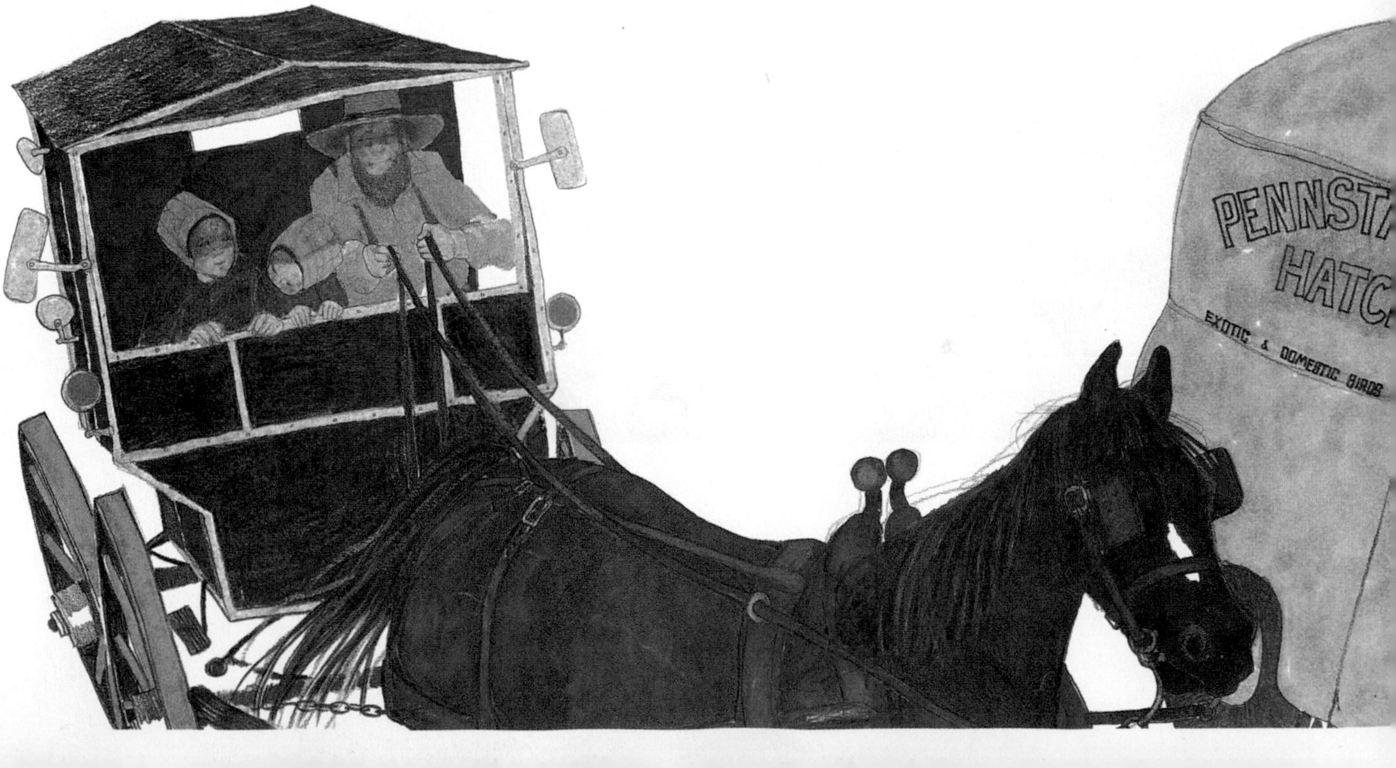

While their father unharnessed and watered the horse, Naomi and Ruth skipped toward the henhouse. The chickens were Naomi's responsibility. She saw to their feeding and watering as well as the collecting of their eggs.

"Everything around here is so plain," Naomi complained. "Our clothes are plain, our houses are plain, even our chickens are plain. It would pleasure me—just once—to have something fancy."

"Shaw, Nomi, you aughtn't to be saying such things," little Ruth scolded.

As Naomi and Ruth searched the field for eggs laid outside the henhouse, they spotted a very unusual one nestled in the tall grass down the drive and behind the henhouse, next to the road.

"This egg looks different from any I have ever seen," Naomi said quietly. "It's still warm—let's put it in Henny's nest. This one needs to be hatched." She gently picked up the egg and eased it into her basket.

Although it was a little bigger than Henny's other eggs and a little darker in color, Naomi gently tucked the egg into the nest while Henny and Ruth looked on.

"You're so good with chickens," Ruth chirped. "I just know you're going to get your white cap this year. Momma says you're ready."

Naomi was proud of her chickens and the way she raised them. The elders were coming for a working bee,

or frolic, in the coming summer. And Naomi wondered whether her parents might present her with the white cap on that day. Her thoughts were interrupted by Ruth's voice.

"Ain't we pleasured," she said. "You wanted something fancy, and now you've got it."

As the days passed, Naomi and Ruth checked Henny's nest constantly. Every day they peered over the edge of the crib, watching for signs of cracks in the shells. Then, one day, the eggs hatched.

"Look at the little chick from the fancy egg, Nomi," Ruth squealed.

"That egg was fancy inside and out, wasn't it?" said Naomi. "Fancy. That's just what we'll name this chick."

"Fancy, Fancy, Fancy, Fancy," Ruth sang out as she jumped about. Naomi smiled and clapped her hands.

All that afternoon, the girls stayed with Henny, watching and studying their special little chick.

Weeks passed. Henny's chicks grew quickly and were soon scratching around in the dirt. They had all lost their yellow down feathers and had grown bright white ones. All of them, except Fancy. Fancy looked very different from the others. There was no doubt about it—this chick wasn't plain!

One afternoon in the washhouse, Naomi and Ruth overheard Aunt Sarai talking to cousin Hannah about a person in the neighboring Amish community.

"She dressed too fancy," Sarai said. "She had to be *shunned*!"

"Is it wrong to be fancy?" Naomi asked.

"Indeed, yes!" snapped Hannah. "We are plain folk. It is in our laws, the *Ordnung*, that we must be plain!"

"What does . . . 'shun' mean?" Ruth asked haltingly.

"Someone who is shunned is shamed in front of the elders. After that, friends and neighbors are instructed not to speak to that person. They are no longer one of us," Sarai answered with authority. Naomi and Ruth looked at each other and hurried outside to hang up the washing. Naomi felt botherment inside.

As soon as they were finished, the girls ran to the henhouse.

"What are we going to do?" Ruth asked. "Fancy is too fancy to be Amish!" Then Fancy ruffled up his feathers and did something that took their breath clean away.

"We'll have to hide him until we know what to do," Naomi said finally. "The elders will be here for the frolic tomorrow."

"He'll be shunned," Ruth whimpered. "Maybe we will be, too!"

They put Fancy into another part of the henhouse and locked the door.

The next morning, the neighboring Amish folk arrived for the frolic. The men and boys helped add a stable onto the Vleckes' barn. They worked hard in the sun while the womenfolk cooked and gossiped. Naomi and Ruth helped

serve the food, pour lemonade, and thread needles for the women who were quilting. This should have been a happy day for them. But the girls were not pleasured because they were sad with worry about Fancy.

When she had served the last ladle of lemonade, Naomi started toward the henhouse. Just then she noticed the open door. But before she could get there to shut it, Fancy darted out and ran toward the gathering, flapping his wings.

"Oh, no!" Naomi called out. "This is all my fault. I wanted something fancy. I should have known better than to make that kind of wish!"

Tears ran down Ruth's cheeks when she saw what had happened. "Poooor Fancy," she cried. "Now he'll be shunned."

Over . . . Under . . . Around . . . Through. . . . Naomi ran after Fancy, trying to catch him before anyone noticed. And that's about the time that Fancy decided to head straight for the elders. He flew at Martha, the oldest member of the gathering. Adjusting her glasses, she gasped as he flew over her head just before landing on the clothesline where the quilts were airing.

"Please don't shun him," Naomi cried. "I did this! I made him fancy," she sobbed. At that moment, pleased with all the attention, Fancy ruffled his feathers and did for the guests what he had done for the girls in the henhouse the day before. Those who weren't speechless were stunned!

"Dry your tears, child." It was Martha who finally spoke. "This isn't your doing. This be God's handiwork. Only He could think up colors like that."

"You mean you aren't going to shun him?" Ruth asked.

"One can only be shunned for going against the ways of our people," Martha continued. "This is no plain old chicken. This be one of God's most beautiful creations. He is fancy, child, and that's the way of it."

All who were gathered there rejoiced in Fancy's beauty. "I believe you have this coming, child," old Martha said as she held out the new white organdy cap. Your family believes you have earned this well. And I agree. Not only have you given good and faithful care to your flock of chickens, but you have also raised one of the finest peacocks I ever did see!"

Standing proudly amidst the gathering, Naomi held Fancy in her arms. She had learned many things that day.

And although no one ever quite knew how Fancy came to be hatched by Henny, it was never questioned. Plainly it was a miracle . . . and sometimes miracles are JUST PLAIN FANCY!

POTATO VACATION

Mary Stolz

illustrated by Pat Doyle

I am a girl, Peggy.

He is my brother. We call him Rusty. He's six and three-quarters and I'm older.

We both go to the same school. It's in town and we have to take a bus to get there. We take a school bus to get to school and a town bus to get to town. Papa has an old car,

but he only takes it to town once a week, when we do the marketing.

We live in a farmhouse, but there's no farm to it now, only an acre and a barn and our house. Once it was a farm, so it's far out in the country which is why you have to take a bus to get anywhere.

There are lots of big and small farms around where we live. Potato farms. Famous potato farms of the state of Maine. There are potato farms in other places, too. The state of Idaho. Maybe some other states.

Around where we live, what people think about is potatoes. I guess there are some other things they think about, but if you ask me, mostly they think about potatoes. Especially in October. Potatoes are how just about everybody around here makes a living.

Around here there's a potato vacation. That means they close the schools for a week when the potatoes are being harvested. Me and my brother gather potatoes then. Of course, the other children get the week off, too. And the teachers, too. They don't all go to the potato fields, but most of them do.

Nobody is rich around here, except a few people. Most of us are poor. Of course, nobody's going to get rich picking potatoes, but you do get paid for doing it. Even kids get paid.

We have to get up very early when we gather potatoes. It's always still dark when we get up, and cold. They have a joke here about Maine and the seasons. They say we have ten months of winter and two months of poor sledding.

We go down in the kitchen where it's warm by the stove. We dress there and have breakfast. Then Momma gives us lunch, to eat in the middle of the morning because we start so early. We each get a box with sandwiches in it, and cookies, and an apple, and some hot cocoa in a thermos.

Then we go out in front of the house and stand by the road in the dark waiting for the potato bus. Shivering. Our dog, Potato Face Sam, waits with us. It seems to me we're always riding buses. The school bus, the town bus, the potato bus. Anyway, the potato bus comes along and takes us to the field where we gather the potatoes.

First the machine goes by and throws the potatoes up out of the ground. Then we gather them and put them in baskets.

In the summer the potato fields are pretty—oh, so pretty. The plants have flowers, some white, some pink, waving for miles in their green leaves. They cover the fields like the pink and white and green patchwork quilt Grandma made for Momma and Papa's room.

But by potato vacation all the flowers are gone, and so are the plants. The farmers spray the plants and that makes them shrivel and die away. By potato vacation all there is are fields of brown ground and potatoes tossed up by the machine.

At first when we get to the field, it's a little bit nice. By then the sky is red as winesap apples and there's a twinkle of frost everywhere and the air is bright and still cold but not so very. I like it then.

What I do not like is gathering potatoes.

I get tired. I know what Grandma means when she says she aches all over. I ache all over by about the fourth potato. Rusty doesn't get nearly as tired as I do, but that's because he's naturally a slow mover. I've got twelve potatoes in our basket by the time he's selected one and dropped it in, careful, as if it mattered where the thing fell.

He's pretty little for potato vacation work and Momma didn't want him to go, but he's stubborn and wouldn't stay behind. Lots of times he wipes a potato off on his shirt and eats it. Just like that. Not washed or cooked or peeled or anything. He says it's as good as an apple, but that's not so. I never eat potatoes.

Potatoes in the field look a lot like stones. It's hard sometimes to tell a stone from a potato before you pick it up, but of course you're supposed to throw a stone back on the ground, not in your basket.

Some kids try to cheat and put stones in their baskets, but practically nobody ever gets away with it. There are overseers everywhere, and they're sharp as axes. I bet they can tell a stone from a potato fifteen rows away in the dark.

I wouldn't dare put a stone in my basket, even if I wanted to cheat, which I do not. I have a friend who says she'd cheat if she dared and she says I would, too. She's wrong, but there's no way to tell her, so I don't bother to try. I know what I know about myself.

Mostly they let the school children go home in the afternoon. If they didn't there'd be a whole field of kids crying. Picking potatoes is just such hard work. I usually feel like crying about the middle of the first basket, but I don't, of course. Rusty would curdle if I cried.

One day I was putting potatoes in our basket. My hands hurt and my back hurt and my nails were all broken and I thought it would be just lovely to cry if Rusty hadn't been there. Then this big frog came along. There was a little frog with him.

"My," I said to the big frog, "what a fine-looking son you have there."

"You're cuckoo," said my brother. "Cuckoo Peggy."

"You'd better go," I said to the frog. "Someone might put you in a basket and sell you for a Maine potato."

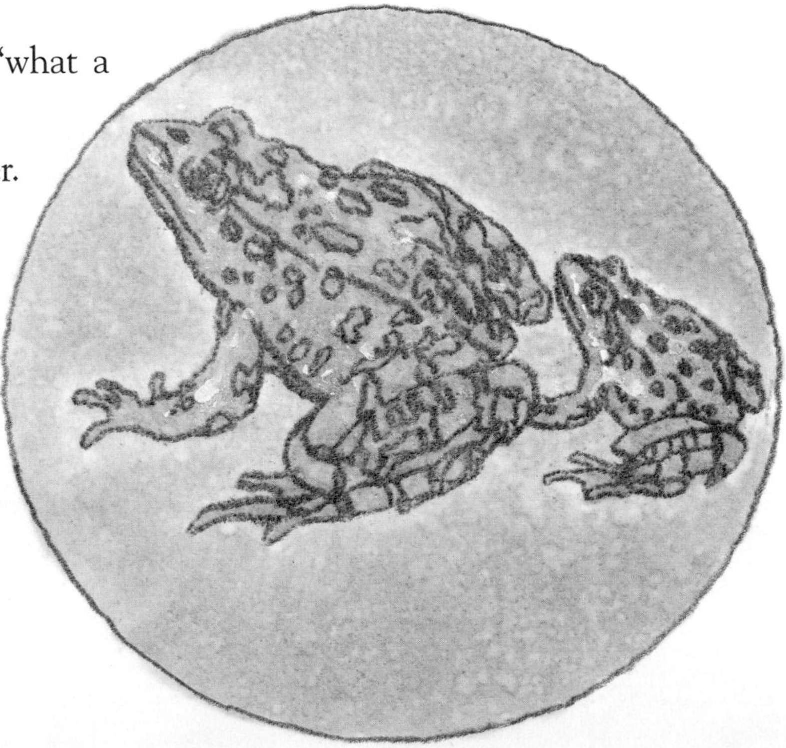

"You're crazy, Peggy!" yelled my brother. "Crazy, crazy!"

But he isn't even seven and he doesn't know that sometimes you have to talk crazy to keep from feeling crazy.

Another time a puppy came running down the row. He had long flopping ears and this skinny long tail. Nobody owned him. I asked everybody, but nobody did. The overseer said to knock it off about the puppy and get back to work. We took the puppy home on the bus with us and Papa said we could keep him. We named him Potato Face Sam, but he only answers to Sam.

Every morning he comes out to the road and waits with us for the bus to come. First the potato bus, and then after that the school bus. When we get home, he's waiting there

again, wagging his skinny tail and barking. Momma says he can tell time, because he always knows when to go out to the road and start waiting and wagging. How does he know? It's a mystery.

I haven't decided what to be when I grow up, but I know one thing. I'm not going to be a potato farmer. I think I'll marry a man who lives in town and then I won't have to wait for a bus to go anywhere. I'll walk around town and if I want to get out of town I'll take an airplane.

This was Rusty's first time picking, and he says he's going to pick potatoes every October all the rest of his life. He says he's going to be a potato farmer when he grows up. But he's only six and three-quarters and doesn't know everything about himself yet.

I really truly do not like potatoes. I don't like to pick them. I never eat them. Just the same, in the summer, when those pink and white flowers in their green leaves are waving in the wind, it's pretty. I don't think I'll ever eat potatoes, but if a potato farmer was really very nice, maybe I'd marry him.

WHAT EVER HAPPENED TO THE BAXTER PLACE?

Pat Ross

illustrated by Roger Duvoisin

Some years ago you could turn off the main road outside a small town in Maryland onto a dirt road which stretched three miles. The old dirt road was called Flatland Road, and it led you straight to the Baxter Place.

It was really a farm belonging to the Baxter family—acres and acres of fields and meadows and woodland—but everybody around just called it the Baxter Place.

A herd of cows grazed in the east meadow. Wild ducks and geese swam in the pond nearby.

Stretching up to a big white farmhouse was a field of soybeans, making a pretty blanket of green in the spring and summer months.

The Baxter Place spread out over nearly three hundred acres. The south field—the biggest and flattest—was planted

in rotation with corn one year and barley the next. The rolling east field was well-suited for alfalfa, giving three cuttings each year. The west field, the smallest stretch, was reserved for crops the Baxters might want for their own, with surplus going for sale.

The fields were divided by woods, like nature's markers.

There were four in the family. Sara Baxter was a big, strong woman with a friendly way, and Pete Baxter was a tall and wiry man with skin toughened and tanned from being outdoors all year round. Sue Ann, the older child, seemed to take after her mother's side of the family. Last there was young Pete, named after his dad, but everybody called him Pee Wee. It's said he was so tiny when he was born that he fit in a shoe box, so Pee Wee they called him, and the name stuck.

The Baxter Place was a business—a farm business. It was also a way of life.

Nothing kept Pete Baxter from the work in the fields or in the big dairy barn that had milking stalls for twenty cows at a time. Pete knew every crop, every one of their hundred cows by name, and everything that happened on the farm. For him, farming was more than any regular full-time job, and he liked being outdoors every day all year round.

Sara Baxter raised chickens in a chicken house. During the laying season, she collected about a hundred eggs every day, then drove them to town to Hammil's Country Market to be sold. She also grew vegetables, and those that didn't get eaten right away got canned and preserved for the long winter or taken to the market along with the eggs. Sara kept careful records of everything that was bought or sold for the farm. She was not only the farm's bookkeeper but also the business-minded one in the family.

Jim and Wally were the hired hands—farmers who work at farming other people's land. Jim was a cracker-jack repairman when the tractor and equipment broke down—which was more often than he liked. And Wally knew the planting seasons like the back of his hand. Folks said he could smell a late spring frost in the air. Both Jim and Wally came every morning at six sharp and often stayed till late in the evening. They had worked with Pete for fifteen years.

Sue Ann did her chores every morning before the school bus came up Flatland Road. She cleaned the calves' stalls, fed the chickens, helped with the milking, and set the table for break-fast—which came *after* chores.

Pee Wee, being younger, got away with a little less in the way of work. He was in charge of feeding the three big watchdogs and an untold number of cats, cleaning the chicken house, and helping Sara set out breakfast for everyone.

All the folks around those parts said the Baxter Place was the prettiest, neatest farm they'd ever seen, and the Baxters were some of the nicest folks they knew. Luckiest, too. And they were right—until the day the man from the market stopped by.

Jess Hammil owned the farmers' market where Sara took her eggs and produce to be sold. Sara, Pete, and Jess had all been in grade school together, so they went way back. Jess came to see the Baxters the day he learned the lease on his small vegetable market in town wasn't going to be renewed. A fancy new building was going up in its place, and he sure couldn't afford those rents.

Now, he figured if he could buy his own land—and not rent—something like this wasn't likely to happen again. He had saved the cash, so maybe the Baxters would be willing to part with that small west field. With those twenty-five acres, Jess could not only have his market, he could also grow much of his own seasonal produce instead of always depending on other farmers. The field was right off the main road from town, so people would be likely to stop and buy.

It was true that particular piece of land was what you might call extra. Sara and Pete had always thought they would save it for Sue Ann and Pee Wee. But Sue Ann was headed for forestry college in a year and planned to move later on to the mountains where her work would be. And Pee Wee, young as he was, had his heart set on being a mathematician, and claimed he was allergic to field work—which certainly seemed to be true!

Jess's being an old friend and all helped the Baxters decide to sell. Also, Sara thought it would be kind of nice to have a market for her sales so close by. They shook hands and made a deal.

Within a year, Jess opened a brand-new market. He planted his land with seasonal produce crops. When word got around that the state was planning to widen and resurface Main Road, Jess knew this meant even more business for him.

Pete and Sara figured they'd not only made some money to pay the bills more easily, but they'd also done a favor for a friend.

Every year for the past five, Emma Price from Homestead Realty Company had made her call on the Baxters. Every year it was the same: Emma's real estate company was interested in purchasing and developing their meadow and woodland area around the pond. Would they consider selling? The offer would be handsome.

Every year they greeted Emma Price politely, but their answer had always been a firm no. They needed the meadow for the cows. And how could they part with the woods and pond? Besides, they didn't need the money. So each year they bade Emma good-by with the same answer.

But one year, things were a little different. The corn harvest that fall had been a total loss. There had been too much rain during planting time and a dry spell just when they needed rain. Corn was their livelihood, and without the crop's sale the bills would go unpaid. Sara figured they could barely pay for the farm's necessities that year. They also owed the bank a mortgage on the house and the land plus money they had borrowed for seed and a new tractor.

They insisted they would not part with the meadow, pond, and woods. Still, they didn't like getting into debt any more if they could help it. Would the Homestead Realty Company consider the rolling east field? they asked. Emma Price was pleasantly surprised and said yes right away.

It was the toughest decision they'd ever had to make together.

Would the company please save some of the trees when they made room for houses? Sue Ann asked. Emma Price assured her they'd make every effort to do just that. Would the Baxters get the best price, even though the east field was the company's second choice? Sara and Pete asked. Emma quoted them a price. Would the new people have children his age? Pee Wee asked. Everyone laughed nervously. Pete quickly figured out loud that they could use the front soybean field for alfalfa, too. There would just be less of a soybean crop, and they would have to sell off some of the older cows in the herd, but the fifty milk-producing cows would not go hungry.

Hurting with the pain of parting with their good land, but having to, the Baxters signed the east field over to Emma Price's company. Homestead Realty paid them without delay. In turn, the Baxters paid for their bad year and looked forward to better ones.

Soon bulldozers were clearing the land, leaving pitifully few of the trees, going against what Emma Price had promised. But it was not all bad, the Baxters told themselves and each other. When the noises and smells of building began to die down, the new houses looked pretty and comfortable, and the people who moved into them seemed friendly enough. It was just strange to see the old alfalfa field planted with so many houses.

Several years of good crops did follow and things seemed to be almost back to normal, even though more and more houses were being built all around. Sue Ann won a partial scholarship to forestry college. Everybody was proud of her, but missed her a lot.

Pee Wee had just started high school when the milking problem came up. Each morning he'd pitch in to take Sue

Ann's place. Jim and Wally still arrived at the crack of dawn, but Jim was getting on in years, and it seemed to take him longer to get the cows milked than it used to. Besides, a lot of the local farmers were putting in new automatic equipment—milking parlors, they called them, with an elevated stall for each cow and tubes leading right to the main tank. The Baxters still relied on the old methods. Not that they wouldn't have changed over. But the cost of the new setup was more than they could swing. So, for a while at least, Pee Wee did his best to help out. Wally never missed a day, but he was no longer up to heavy work, so Sara pitched in more often.

Still, it got harder and harder to compete with the milk production of neighboring farmers who had installed milking parlors to handle larger herds in less time than it took the Baxters. Milk sales were barely bringing in enough to cover costs, so it wasn't long before the Baxters began to sell off the rest of their herd.

Finally, only five cows grazed in the meadow. The milking barn was practically empty. And even though the Baxters didn't have their herd, they took comfort in knowing that the milk and butter on their kitchen table was not store-bought, but still their own.

The following spring George Stillwell came to see Pete and Sara Baxter about using the pond and meadow area for sports land. He didn't want to *buy* the land—which pleased the Baxters, as they'd made up their minds they'd never part with the pond. George Stillwell proposed leasing the area for eight years. He would put up what he called a "rustic cabin" and, in turn, rent it out to hunters during the fall and winter gunning seasons.

Pete figured that was a good enough deal. The pond was a safe distance from the housing development. Besides, the whole area filled up with hunters during the duck and goose seasons anyway. The Baxters had always let some hunters on their land, so a few more couldn't do much harm, except for the noise. And without actually giving up the land, they would be paid for it. This would fill the hole in their pockets left by the loss of milk money, and would help to fill Pee Wee's college savings account. So Sara, too, reluctantly agreed.

In the next year, the cabin, only a little bigger than the Baxters had expected, went up. They could live with a few hunters for eight years.

Pee Wee, now Petie to everyone except his family, went off to engineering school a whole year ahead of his

graduating class. This came as no great surprise to the Baxters, and his ambitions made them proud.

Jim retired officially, but still came around to tinker with the machinery and complain how the new tractor wasn't up to the old model.

Again, things returned almost to normal. Pete and Sara had a smaller place, but it was plenty for them and Wally to handle. They still had the big south field for corn and barley, and the front field for other crops. Sara had her chickens and her garden. Life on the farm was different, what with the changes and Sue Ann and Pee Wee away most of the year. Perhaps now things would stay put for a while. And they did in fact—for some time.

But things once set out of order never quite stay put for long.

One day something happened that the Baxters found hard to understand. Jess Hammil sold out to a developer, a big developer.

Jess's country market and his land were bulldozed to make Main Shopping Mall, featuring a giant supermarket, a discount drugstore, a dress boutique, a chain department store, and countless other small shops.

Not long after this, Homestead Realty Company made the Baxters an offer on the big south field. This time they didn't *have* to sell, but Wally was about to retire and Pete and Sara were no longer up to heavy work. They could look for new hired hands, but it just didn't seem the same. The offer was tempting, so they finally accepted.

One thing led to another. The man who'd rented the pond made an offer to buy now that the lease was about to expire. Since the pond and meadow would never be the

same again, what with a shopping center bordering it, the Baxters could see little reason to hold onto it. It had lost almost all its meaning for them.

After the sale to George Stillwell—the most profitable and the most heartbreaking for the Baxters—the cabin was turned into Rustic Manor Motor Lodge and Tennis Club almost overnight.

The Baxter Place was not even half of what it had been not too many years before. But the trees—those that were left—still acted as dividers, trying hard to keep the Baxter Place separate.

Sara and Pete still had the front field leading up to the old farmhouse. In the early years, they had had to struggle hard just to make the place pay for itself. Now they had some money in the bank. That was something.

Folks couldn't still say the Baxter Place was the prettiest, neatest place around—not the way it had gotten so divided up and changed. But folks could still say the Baxters were some of the nicest folks they'd ever known. And they were. That had not changed. But so many things *had*.

"What ever happened to the old Baxter Place?" somebody asked. And nobody could quite say. Not even the Baxters.

HOW DOES THE GARDEN GROW?

from EARLY FARM LIFE by Lise Gunby

illustrated by Jane Kendall

Does your family have a vegetable garden? Do you grow all the vegetables you put on your dinner table? Perhaps you grow only the vegetables you especially like and buy the rest at a store. There were no large grocery stores where the settlers could buy fresh food. If they wanted vegetables they had to grow their own.

The early farmer's garden was much larger than most gardens today. Farmers had to plant, weed, and harvest all the vegetables they needed for the entire year!

COLLECTING THE SEEDS

Farmers could not go to the local nursery to buy seeds and seedlings the way we do. Settlers brought seeds with them to plant in their gardens. Neighbors traded with each other to get new varieties of plants. After the first harvest, families collected seeds from their own vegetables. The seeds were separated and carefully dried. Then they were wrapped in newspaper or cloth and tied with string. The

names of the seeds were written on the containers. If the seeds were mixed up, the garden would be unpredictable next summer! The seeds had to be stored in a very dry place until the spring. If the seeds were carelessly put in a damp place, they would rot.

THE COMPOST HEAP

Early farmers could not buy chemical fertilizers for their gardens. They made their own fertilizers to be sure that the nutrients used by plants were replaced. A family made a compost heap. The word *compost* means a mixture. The compost was heaped into a wooden bin and kept in the shade of the house. The early farmers did not waste anything! They threw egg shells, pumpkin rinds, potato peels, and the rest of their table scraps into the compost heap. All organic leftovers and garbage were put into the bin. Do you know what happened next? All of these scraps slowly decomposed into a rich fertilizer. In the spring, the

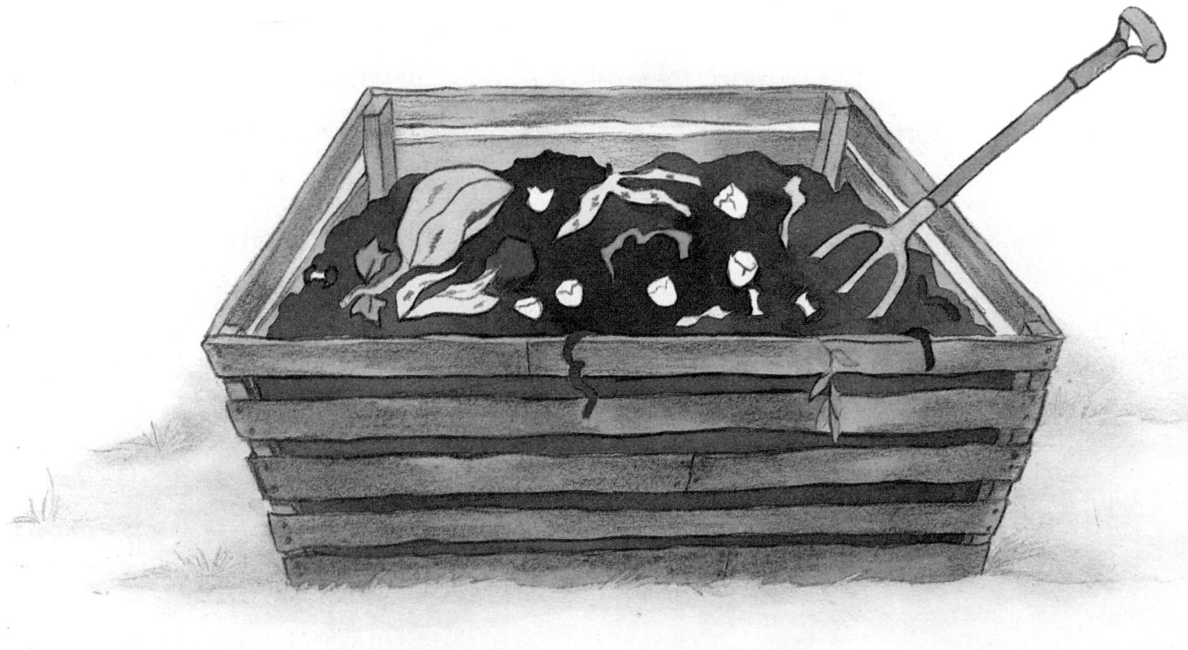

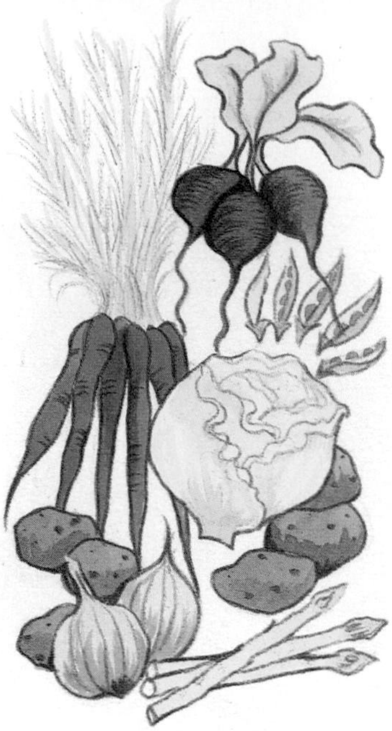

farmer mixed some manure with this compost and spread the fertilizer over the garden soil. The garden plants loved this organic food!

Settlers loved vegetables. The farm kitchen was no place for picky eaters. The farm family planted onions, parsnips, lettuce, peas, beans, asparagus, cabbage, beets, carrots, cucumbers, and lots and lots of potatoes. Potatoes were a staple food.

For many years settlers thought tomatoes were poisonous. They grew them in their gardens as a decoration, but did not eat them. Later they realized that tomatoes were not only safe, but tasty. The early farmers planted extra pumpkin and squash patches where they grew feed for their cattle and pigs.

SPICES AND SEASONINGS

Early farmers could not buy spices and seasonings. They grew their own herbs and spices in their gardens. Do you recognize any of the following herbs: rue, thyme, sage, rosemary, savory, fennel, caraway, wormwood, lovage, or pennyroyal? These are some of the flavorful herbs the settlers added to their soups and stews. In the fall, when the herbs were ripe, the farmers picked and dried them. They hung them in little bunches from the pantry ceiling where they were handy to the cook.

The settlers protected their food. Every country garden was surrounded by a sturdy fence to keep out the chickens, pigs, cattle, and rabbits which loved to nibble on the little green shoots. Children enjoyed making a scarecrow to fool the wild pests who could fly over the fence. The fence was lined with hollyhocks, gooseberry, raspberry, and currant bushes.

PRIVATE PATCHES FOR THE CHILDREN

Children helped to tend the garden. Often each child had a private vegetable patch. Children planted the vegetables that they loved best in these little plots. Learning to grow vegetables was an important skill. Do you think you would like your own vegetable patch? Imagine watching vegetables grow from tiny seeds into full-grown plants. What vegetables would you plant in your garden?

THE COUNTRY MOUSE AND THE CITY MOUSE

from AESOP'S FABLES
illustrated by Heidi Holder

An honest, plain, sensible Country Mouse invited her city friend for a visit. When the City Mouse arrived, the Country Mouse opened her heart and hearth in honor of her old friend. There was not a morsel that she did not bring forth out of her larder—peas and barley, cheese parings and nuts—hoping by quantity to make up for what she feared was wanting in quality, eating nothing herself, lest her guest should not have enough. The City Mouse, condescending to pick a bit here and a bit there, at length exclaimed, "My dear, please let me speak freely to you. How can you endure the dullness of your life here, with nothing but woods and meadows, mountains and brooks about? You can't really prefer these empty fields to streets teeming with carriages and men! Do you not long for the conversation of the world instead of the chirping of birds? I promise you will find the city a change for the better. Let's away this moment!"

Overpowered with such fine words and so polished a manner, the Country Mouse agreed, and they set out on their journey. About midnight they entered a great house, where the City Mouse lived. Here were couches of crimson velvet, ivory carvings, and on the table were the remains of a splendid banquet. The Country Mouse was placed in the midst of a rich Persian carpet, and it was now the turn of the City Mouse to play hostess. She ran to and fro to supply all her guest's wants, serving dish upon dish and dainty upon dainty. The Country Mouse sat and enjoyed herself, delighted with this new turn of affairs. Just as she was thinking with contempt of the poor life she had forsaken, the door flew open and a noisy party burst into the room. The frightened friends scurried for the first corner they could find. No sooner did they peek out than the barking of dogs drove them back in greater terror than before. At length, when things seemed quiet, the Country Mouse stole from her hiding place and bade her friend good-bye, whispering, "Oh, my dear, this fine mode of living may do for you, but I prefer my poor barley in peace and quiet to dining at the richest feast where Fear and Danger lie waiting."

A simple life in peace and safety is preferable to a life of luxury tortured by fear.

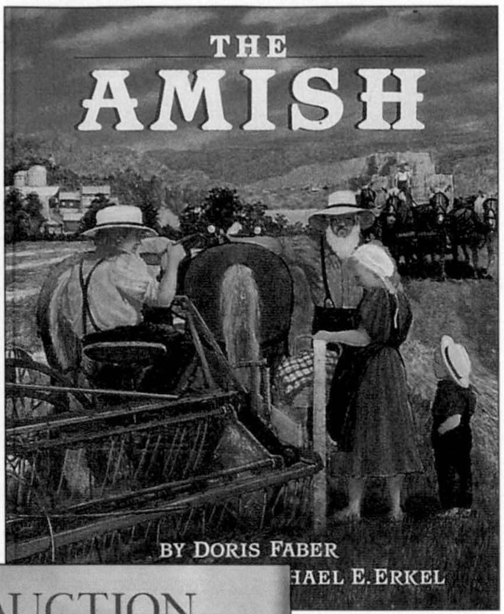

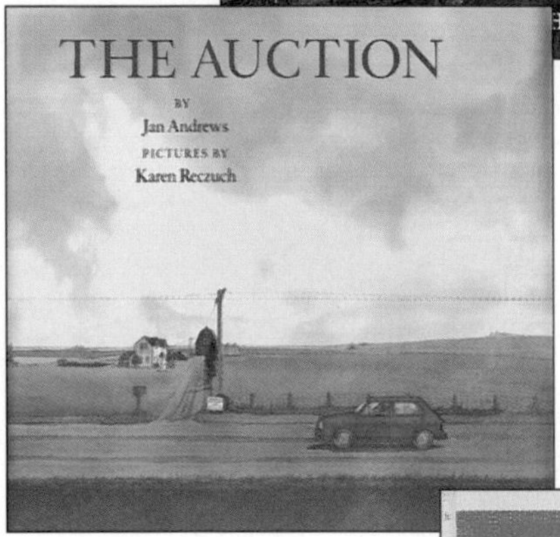

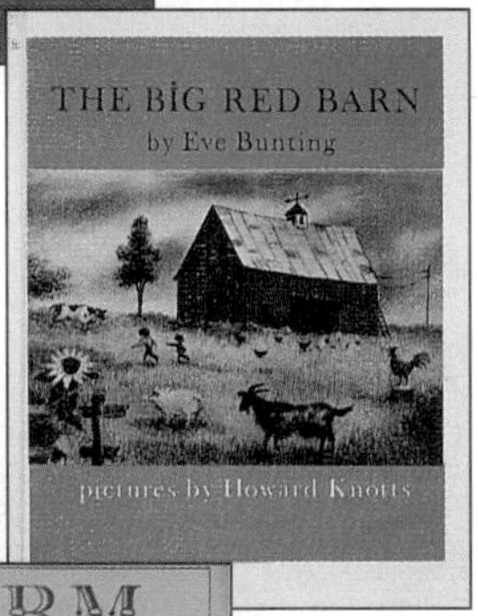

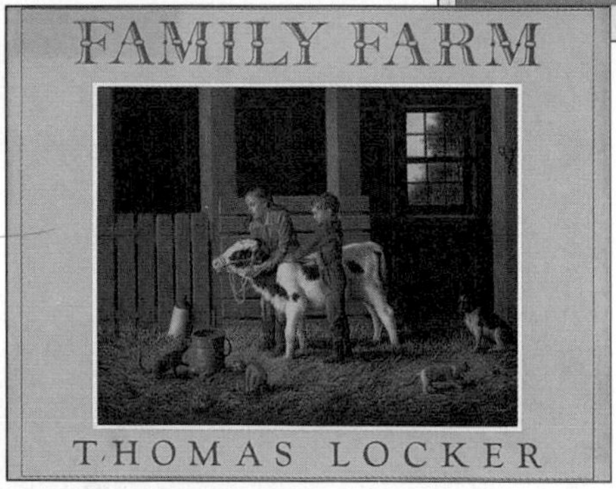

BIBLIOGRAPHY

The Amish by Doris Faber.
Here's a great explanation of the history, life style, and future of the Amish people.

The Auction by Jan Andrews.
Todd and his grandfather share their feelings and memories as they spend a last night together on the family farm before it is auctioned off.

The Big Red Barn by Eve Bunting.
A young farm girl, who knows how important the farm's big red barn is to her, learns to accept the many changes that must take place—not only on the farm but in her life as well.

Family Farm by Thomas Locker.
Many small family farms today are failing. How will the family in this story save their failing farm?

Farming the Land: Modern Farmers and Their Machines by Jerry Bushey. Here's another book about modern farming methods and the machines that today's farmers use.

Farming Today Yesterday's Way by Cheryl Walsh Bellville. Spend a year on a small dairy farm in Wisconsin where workhorses, rather than machines, do most of the work.

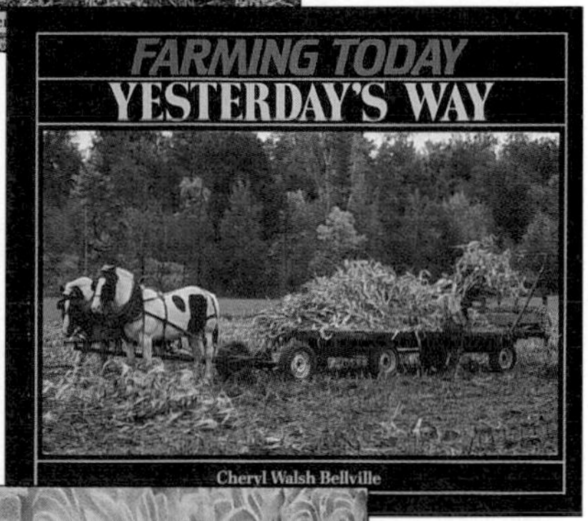

Jamie's Turn by Jamie DeWitt. Jamie, a real farm boy from Wisconsin, tells how he rescued his stepfather after an accident with farm machinery and how he ran the farm for nearly a year while his stepfather recovered.

Our Vanishing Farm Animals: Saving America's Rare Breeds by Catherine Paladino. Find out about some farm animals that are in danger of becoming extinct and the families who are trying to protect them.

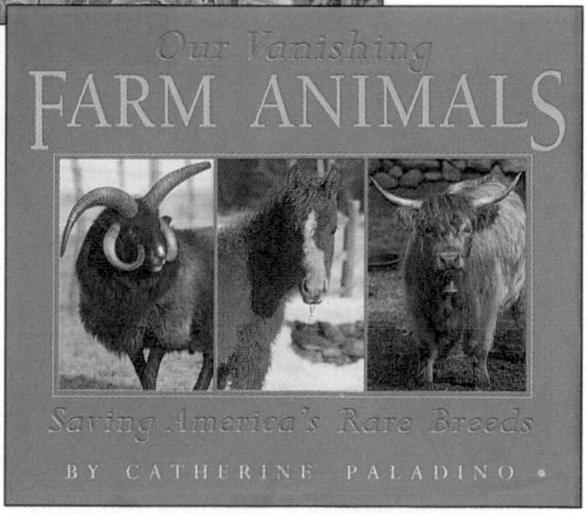

EDWARD MILLER

CITY WILDLIFE

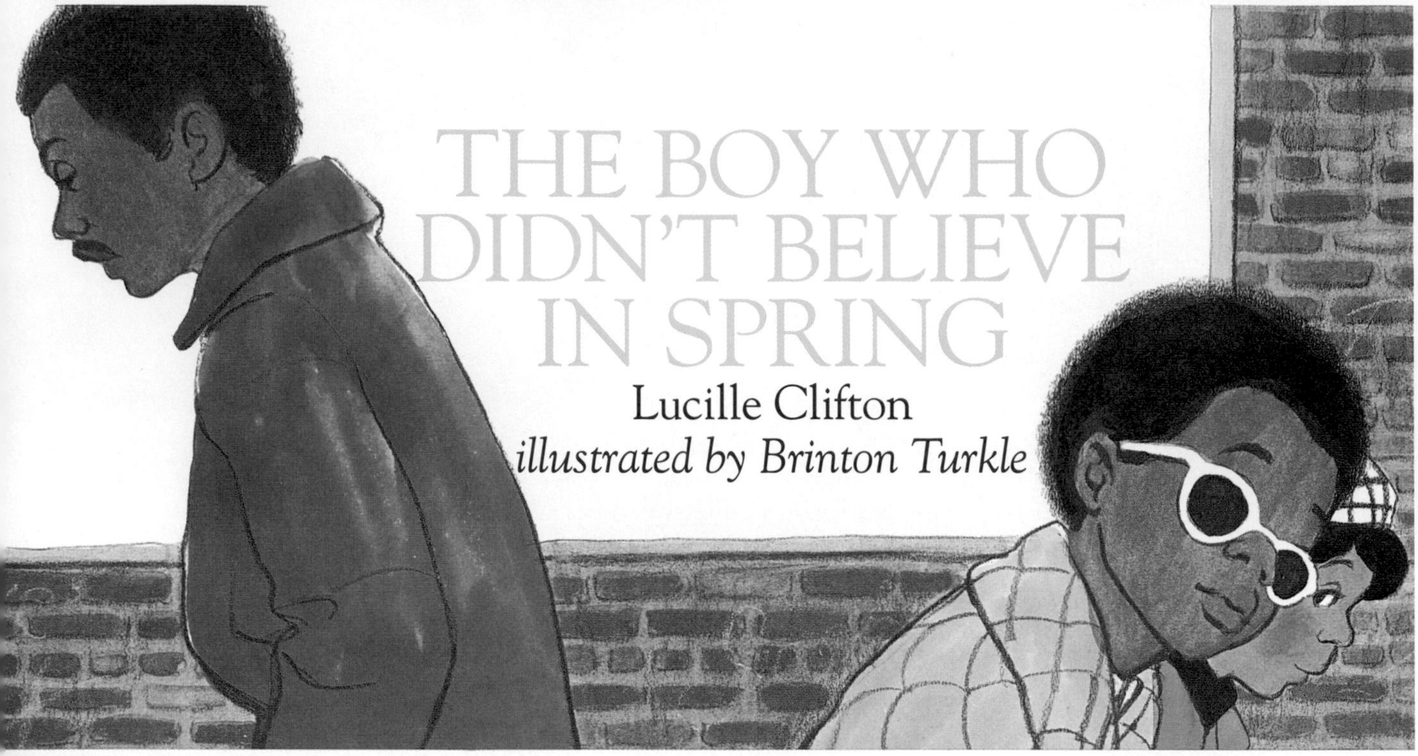

THE BOY WHO DIDN'T BELIEVE IN SPRING

Lucille Clifton

illustrated by Brinton Turkle

Once upon a time there was a little boy named King Shabazz who didn't believe in Spring.

"No such thing!" he would whisper every time the teacher talked about Spring in school.

"Where is it at?" he would holler every time his Mama talked about Spring at home.

He used to sit with his friend Tony Polito on the bottom step when the days started getting longer and warmer and talk about it.

"Everybody talkin bout Spring!" he would say to Tony.

"Big deal," Tony would say back.

"No such thing!" he would say to Tony.

"Right!" Tony would say back.

One day after the teacher had been talking about birds that were blue and his Mama had started talking about crops coming up, King Shabazz decided he had just had enough. He put his jacket on and his shades and went by for Tony Polito.

"Look here, man," King said when they got out to the bottom step, "I'm goin to get me some of this Spring."

"What you mean, man?" Tony asked him.

"Everybody talkin bout Spring comin, and Spring just round the corner. I'm goin to go round there and see what do I see."

Tony Polito watched King Shabazz get up and push his shades up tight on his nose.

"You comin with me, man?" he said while he was pushing.

Tony Polito thought about it for a minute. Then he got up and turned his cap around backwards.

"Right!" Tony Polito said back.

King Shabazz and Tony Polito had been around the corner before, but only as far as the streetlight alone. They passed the school and the playground.

"Aint no Spring in there," said King Shabazz with a laugh. "Sure aint," agreed Tony Polito.

They passed Weissman's. They stopped for a minute by the side door at Weissman's and smelled the buns.

"Sure do smell good," whispered Tony.

"But it aint Spring," King was quick to answer.

They passed the apartments and walked fast in case they met Junior Williams. He had said in school that he was going to beat them both up.

Then they were at the streetlight. Tony stopped and made believe his sneaker was untied to see what King was going to do. King stopped and blew on his shades to clean them and to see what Tony was going to do. They stood there for two light turns and then King Shabazz grinned at Tony Polito, and he grinned back, and the two boys ran across the street.

"Well, if we find it, it ought to be now," said King.

Tony didn't say anything. He just stood looking around.

"Well, come on, man," King whispered, and they started down the street.

They passed the Church of the Solid Rock with high windows all decorated and pretty.

They passed a restaurant with little round tables near the window. They came to a take-out shop and stood by the door a minute to smell the bar-b-q.

"Sure would like to have some of that," whispered King.

"Me too," whispered Tony with his eyes closed. They walked slower down the street.

Just after they passed some apartments King Shabazz and Tony Polito came to a vacant lot. It was small and had high walls from apartments on three sides of it. Three walls around it and right in the middle—a car!

It was beautiful. The wheels were gone and so were the doors, but it was dark red and sitting high on a dirt mound in the middle of the lot.

"Oh man, oh man," whispered King.

"Oh man," whispered Tony.

Then they heard the noise.

It was a little long sound, like smooth things rubbing against rough, and it was coming from the car. It happened again. King looked at Tony and grabbed his hand.

"Let's see what it is, man," he whispered. He thought Tony would say no and let's go home.

Tony looked at King and held his hand tightly.

"Right," he said very slowly.

The boys stood there a minute, then began tiptoeing over toward the car. They walked very slowly across the lot. When they were halfway to the car, Tony tripped and almost fell. He looked down and saw a patch of little yellow pointy flowers, growing in the middle of short spiky green leaves.

"Man, I think you tripped on these crops!" King laughed.

"They're comin up," Tony shouted. "Man, the crops are comin up!"

And just as Tony was making all that noise, they heard another noise, like a lot of things waving in the air, and they looked over at the car and three birds flew out of one of the door holes and up to the wall of the apartment.

King and Tony ran over to the car to see where the birds had been. They had to climb up a little to get to the door and look in.

They stood there looking a long time without saying anything. There on the front seat down in a whole lot of cottony stuff was a nest. There in the nest were four light blue eggs. Blue. King took off his shades.

"Man, it's Spring," he said almost to himself.

"Anthony Polito!"

King and Tony jumped down off the mound. Somebody was shouting for Tony as loud as he could.

"Anthony Polito!"

The boys turned and started walking out of the vacant lot. Tony's brother Sam was standing at the edge of the lot looking mad.

"Ma's gonna kill you, after I get finished, you squirt!" he hollered.

King Shabazz looked at Tony Polito and took his hand.

"Spring is here," he whispered to Tony.

"Right," whispered Tony Polito back.

MEET LUCILLE CLIFTON, AUTHOR

Lucille Clifton says her children helped her with her writing, especially her writing of children's books. She believes they kept her aware of life. "And you have to stay aware of life, keep growing to write," she says.

MEET BRINTON TURKLE, ILLUSTRATOR

Brinton Turkle is a well-known author and illustrator, but The Boy Who Didn't Believe in Spring *was a new challenge for him. He had to do as much research for this story as for some of his historical books. "I've had to study many things I've always taken for granted or ignored," he said. This book "has helped me rediscover New York, sketching boys' jackets, tennis shoes, buses, traffic lights, street signs."*

©Lee Balterman/MGA PHOTRI

CITY LOTS:
LIVING THINGS IN VACANT SPOTS

Phyllis S. Busch

illustrated by Pamela Carroll

Cities are full of buildings—all kinds of buildings. There are big homes and small ones, where people live. There are factories and offices where people work. There are schools, libraries, museums, where people learn.

Cities are also full of people. There are homemakers, housepainters, streetcleaners, shopkeepers, factory workers, firefighters, carpenters, clerks, bankers, bakers, and all their children.

But among this mass of people and their dwellings you can find some vacant spots—large or small places where there are neither people nor buildings. These are known as city lots.

Is there a city lot near where you live? Perhaps you use it as a short cut to a friend's house, or to a store, or to a bus stop.

Some city lots are just narrow shaded passageways between two buildings. Others are bright and sunny. You can find these lots on street corners, or where there are large spaces between buildings.

Was the lot in your neighborhood always vacant? Or was there once a building which was torn down? You might search for evidence such as bricks or pieces of plaster. But first make sure that the lot is a safe place to play this game of exploration.

A vacant lot is really not vacant at all. It is a place where many plants and animals live all year round. A vacant lot contains all the things plants and animals need in order to live: soil, water, air, sunlight, food, space. Here you can watch the changes that take place in living things all through the year.

In the corner of an old city lot you may find a London plane tree, also known as a sycamore. This tree has surprises for every season. In the bright spring sunshine, the brown and tan trunk is a sparkling patchwork of colors. The bark peelings which cause this colorful pattern lie scattered on the ground.

Examine these before and after a rain. You will discover that the tight bark rolls are brittle in dry weather, and loose and softened when it is wet. In the summer it is pleasant to sit in the shade of a sycamore tree, under its spreading dark green leaves. Take the temperature of the air under the tree. How is it different from the temperature of the air in the sunlight?

©E. R. Degginger/Earth Scenes

With the coming of autumn the sycamore leaves turn brown and fall to the ground to form a crunchy carpet. Remove a leaf not yet fallen and find the little hollow at the end of the leaf stalk. Notice how this forms a cap over a new bud—a little bundle of energy ready to start next year's growth.

Winter is the time to see the sycamore balls hanging high in the tree. A strong wind dashes them to the ground, where you can collect some and observe their seeds. How many seeds does one of these balls of fruit contain? How many trees might develop from all the seeds of one parent tree? It is a wonder that the lot is not full of sycamores.

You can also follow the seasons with the ailanthus tree, the commonest city tree. In China, where it came from, it is known as the Tree-of-Heaven. Observe it after the leaves have fallen as it stands with its stout bare branches outstretched against the sky. Large heartshaped scars show where the leaves were attached. You might see bunches of fruit up in the tree, and hear them rattle in the breeze.

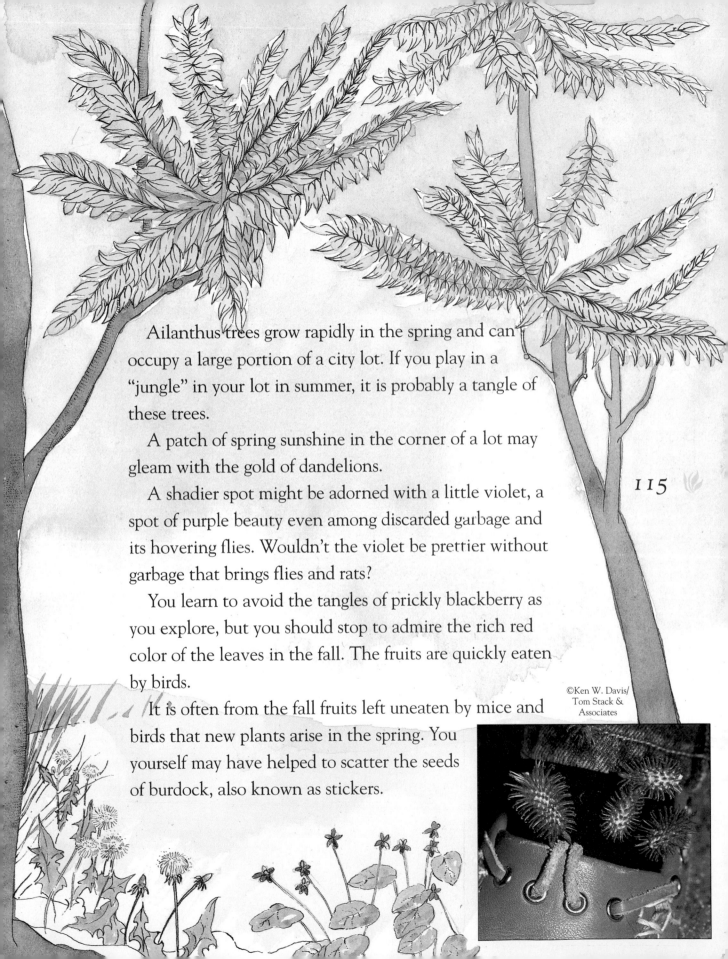

Ailanthus trees grow rapidly in the spring and can occupy a large portion of a city lot. If you play in a "jungle" in your lot in summer, it is probably a tangle of these trees.

A patch of spring sunshine in the corner of a lot may gleam with the gold of dandelions.

A shadier spot might be adorned with a little violet, a spot of purple beauty even among discarded garbage and its hovering flies. Wouldn't the violet be prettier without garbage that brings flies and rats?

You learn to avoid the tangles of prickly blackberry as you explore, but you should stop to admire the rich red color of the leaves in the fall. The fruits are quickly eaten by birds.

It is often from the fall fruits left uneaten by mice and birds that new plants arise in the spring. You yourself may have helped to scatter the seeds of burdock, also known as stickers.

©Ken W. Davis/ Tom Stack & Associates

Run your finger up the stalk of the common plantain when it is wet. Feel the sticky seeds. All who walk over the flat-leaved plantains carry with them some seeds which are later dropped to grow into next year's crop.

©Rod Planck/Tom Stack & Associates

It is fun to spend a year watching any one plant, and milkweed is a happy choice. Milkweed pods are beautiful whether they are open or closed. Look inside a bright green pod in early autumn. See how the many brown seeds with their silvery parachutes fit neatly into a package.

©K. King/PHOTRI

Later in the season all the fruit pods, now in shades of tan, are open. Watch the seeds float in the air on a windy day. Which way do the beautiful wisps travel? How far do they go? Will they give rise to more milkweed plants next spring? What insects will be attracted to their fragrant lavender flowers in summer?

In autumn a city lot is bound to have some tall flourishing ragweed. Although the flowers are tiny, hayfever sufferers know when the plant is in bloom. Large amounts of pollen float in the air and disturb sensitive noses. Shake some flowers over a piece of glass which is covered with a thin layer of petroleum jelly. You can then observe this flower dust under a microscope. The flowers look like miniature sculptures.

Where ragweed grows you might find a corner made bright with purple asters and yellow goldenrod.

If city lots have plants they certainly must have animals. Some insects lay their eggs in the stems of goldenrod. This causes the plant to form a swelling known as a gall. Here the young develop, to hatch out the following spring. If you cut open a gall, you may find an immature insect.

©Doug Sokell/Tom Stack & Associates

Is there a wild black cherry tree on the lot? In the spring you might find a mass of tent caterpillars resting in a silken shelter which they have spun between supporting branches. These insects appear to have regular periods for feeding and for spinning. Observe a colony of tent caterpillars over the weeks in order to learn their routine.

©Donald Specker/Animals Animals

Those caterpillars which are not gobbled up by hungry birds or destroyed by parasites change into brown moths. Look for their shiny dark brown bands of eggs on bare winter twigs.

©Larry Brock/Tom Stack & Associates

Small green plant lice or aphids are frequently found feeding on the juices of stems or leaves. A praying mantis might stalk nearby, gobbling up these and other insects. The praying mantis is a large green and brown insect whose bent front legs make it appear as if it is praying. You can locate its hard brown egg mass among the winter shrubs. Over three hundred babies may hatch from one such egg case in the spring.

A city lot is a suitable habitat for many birds. They need a safe place to build a nest, as well as an adequate food supply and a source of water. Most common is the English sparrow. Observe it as it hops, flies, builds a nest, sits on its eggs, feeds spiders and flies to its young, bathes in rain pools and dusts in sandy spots.

Try to follow the habits of the pigeons which are sure to be there. Maybe there is also a robin, attracted to the cherries in the cherry tree. Are there some squawking starlings? They lead busy lives too.

Did you ever visit the lot during or after a light rainfall in spring or summer? It smells different from the rest of the city—cool and refreshing. How much cooler the air is over the lot than over the pavement. Feel the gentle raindrops on your face. Open your mouth and taste some fresh rainwater. Watch the rain strike the leaves, run down the stalks and onto the stems from where it slowly continues down into the soil. Here is where it is available to the plant roots which absorb it. Miniature streams and lakes form where there are depressions in the ground. Perhaps a puppy or a bird comes for a drink or a bath, leaving its footprints in the mud nearby.

People need places to live, to work, and to shop. But people also need open spaces. Every neighborhood should have a lot which is left without buildings—a place to rest and to play and to make new discoveries about its plants and animals.

LINNEA'S ALMANAC: JANUARY

Christina Björk
illustrated by Lena Anderson

Hi! My name is Linnea. I am named after the linnaea, a little pink woodland flower. I'm no woodland flower, though—I'm an asphalt flower. I live right in the middle of the city, but I love plants and flowers and everything that grows. So a city isn't such a great place for someone like me, right? Wrong. All over my room, things are growing.

My friend Mr. Bloom taught me all about plants. He's a retired gardener who lives in my building. Mr. Bloom has a green thumb. It's not actually green. That just means he's good at making things grow.

For Christmas I got a book called *The Old Farmer's Almanac*. I use it almost every day. It tells you what time the sun will rise and set, when you can see the moon and the planets, and when to expect a comet. There is a weather forecast for the whole year, with dates for the first and last frost. You can write down what the weather is really like, and see if the book is correct.

And now I'll tell you about some of my year, what I did and what I observed. Seasons are not the same everywhere.

The farther south you are, the earlier spring comes, for example. But this is what it's like where *I* live.

When it's cold and snowing outside, I always wonder how the birds will find anything to eat. This year I decided to help out by opening a bird restaurant. There are different things on the menu. But once I start, I've got to keep it up all winter, because the birds get used to it and forget how to find food by themselves. I wonder who will come to my restaurant . . .

Remember: Never *stop* feeding the birds until winter is over. But don't *start* too early either, because then you might fool some migratory birds into staying, and they can't stand the cold. I usually start around Christmastime (a little earlier if it's really cold).

In the city, you can't put out food for the birds on the ground (then the rats come), so I feed them from my window.

Birdhouses aren't as good as bird feeders, where the birds can sit around the edge without getting their droppings into the food. Bird droppings can spread diseases, such as salmonellosis (food poisoning), that birds most often die of.

Seeds for a feeder are sold at plant nurseries, pet stores, or supermarkets.

Feeders have to be refilled every now and then.

Pigeons, crows, magpies, and gulls eat everything they're offered.

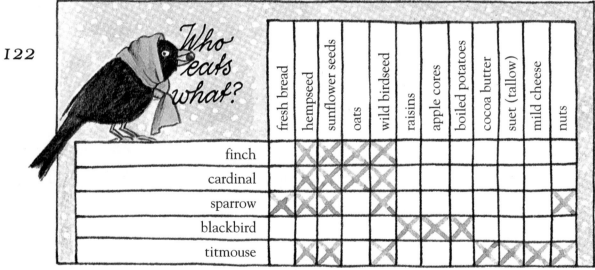

	fresh bread	hempseed	sunflower seeds	oats	wild birdseed	raisins	apple cores	boiled potatoes	cocoa butter	suet (tallow)	mild cheese	nuts
finch		X	X	X	X							
cardinal		X	X	X	X							
sparrow	X	X	X		X							X
blackbird						X	X	X				
titmouse		X	X		X				X	X	X	X

Other bird goodies:
unshelled peanuts, apple cores, coconut halves, or nuts (in a plastic net) on a string.

Dangerous for birds:
moldy, spicy or salty foods!

If you think how warm a down jacket is, then you'll understand how warmly "dressed" birds are with all their down and feathers. But the smaller a bird is, the more it has to eat to survive the winter. A little bird has to eat twice its weight every day. That much "fuel" is needed to keep its tiny body warm.

In the winter, food is hard to find. There are no insects (they're sleeping), no seeds (they're buried under the snow), and no water (it's turned to ice).

That's why many birds fly to warmer places for the winter. But some stay, in spite of everything. They've learned survival tricks, such as moving into the city and getting on "bird welfare" in the parks and by the water, where they are fed.

I usually go to one place where the water never freezes. Seven sacks of food are put out for the birds there every day during the colder months. But the sacks are not filled just with bread crumbs—that would make the birds sick. Birdseed, suet, and lime are added, so the birds will get their vitamins.

I usually bring my own bag with fresh bread, boiled potatoes, chopped white cabbage or lettuce, and birdseed.

Some birds are marked with a numbered band on one leg. That way you can see if the same bird returns year after year. One swan came back every year for twenty years! But that was a record for swans.

Feed water birds in the water!
Don't try to get them to come up on land, where they can be run over.

FLY HIGH FLY LOW

Don Freeman

In the beautiful city of San Francisco, a city famous for its fogs and flowers, cable cars and towers, there once stood an electric-light sign on top of a tall building, and inside the letter B of this sign there lived a pigeon.

Before choosing to make his home here this proud gray pigeon had tried living in many other letters in the alphabet. Just why he liked the lower loop of the letter B, no one yet knew.

During the day the wide side walls kept the wind away, and at night the bright lights kept him warm and cozy.

The pigeons who roosted along the ledges of the building across the street thought he was a pretty persnickety pigeon to live where he did. "He's too choosy! He's too choosy!" they would coo.

The only one who never made fun of him was a white-feathered dove. She felt sure he must have a good reason for wanting to live in that letter.

Every morning as soon as the sun came up, these two met in mid-air and together they swerved and swooped down into Union Square Park, where they pecked up their breakfast. Mr. Hi Lee was certain to be there, throwing out crumbs from his large paper sack. He would always greet them by saying, "Good morning, Sid and Midge. How are my two early birds?"

All the birds in the city regarded Mr. Hi Lee as their best friend, and he had nicknames for many of them. Sometimes he brought them hard breadcrumbs and sometimes, as an extra-special treat, day-old cake crumbs from a nearby bakery.

After every crumb was pecked up, the pigeons always circled around Mr. Hi Lee's head, flapping their wings as they flew—which was their way of saying, "Thank you!"

By noontime Sid and Midge could be seen sailing high in the sky, flying into one cloud and out the other. Side by side they glided over the bay, until they could look down and see the Golden Gate Bridge.

Sid would swoop and fly through the open arches just to show Midge what a good looper he was.

Then, as the setting sun began painting the sky with a rosy glow, two tuckered-out birds would be slowly winging their way back to the park just in time for supper.

One evening after an especially gay lark in the sky, Sid invited Midge to stay and share his letter B with him.

Across the way pigeons were soon bobbing their heads up and down and cooing, "Whoever heard of birds building a nest in a sign? It'll never do! It'll never do!"

But Sid and Midge went right on building their nest as best they could. They used patches of cloth and strands of string and bits of straw, and gradually there grew a strong nest with a perfect view.

Then one misty morning a few weeks later, just as everything was going along smoothly, something happened which was very upsetting! It occurred right after Sid had flown down to the park to peck up his breakfast.

As usual he had left Midge taking her turn sitting on the nest, where there were now two eggs to be kept warm!

Suddenly, like a bolt out of the blue, Midge felt their perch give a terrible lurch! The buildings across the way seemed to sway back and forth. “It’s an earthquake!” screeched Midge.

But no—it was even worse than an earthquake! Their sign was being taken down! One by one the letters were being lowered into a waiting truck below.

Midge followed, flapping her wings wildly at the movers, trying to let them know they must not take away her nest! But the men paid no attention to her, until the tallest man stopped and shouted, “Hold everything!

Look here what I've found! Two eggs in a nest! No wonder that pigeon has been making such a fuss!"

"Well, what do you know!" exclaimed another man as he took a peek inside. "We'll sure have to take good care of this letter. Come to think of it, I know of a bakery shop that could use a big letter B. Anyway, we won't be throwing this one away. Come on, men, let's get going!"

Down the hill they went, and far out of sight, with Midge clinging on with all her might!

You can imagine how Sid felt when he landed back on the cold and empty scaffold later that morning! He stood there dazed and bewildered, wondering where his sign had gone. Where was his Midge? And where, oh where, was their nest with those two precious eggs?

He looked around on all sides, but not a trace of his sign did he see. Suddenly off he flew.

First to the waterfront. Possibly the sign was being loaded onto a boat. Sid was sure that wherever that particular letter B was, there, too, Midge would be. He looked high and he looked low, but not a sign of his letter did he spy.

Next he flew to the uppermost post of the Golden Gate Bridge. He thought perhaps Midge might have passed by that way. But no, not a feather did he find.

While he stood wondering where to search next, an enormous fog bank came rolling in from off the ocean. Like a rampaging flock of sheep, the fog came surging straight toward him!

When Sid saw this he puffed out his chest and stretched his wings wide and cried, "Who's afraid of a little breeze? I'll flap my wings and blow the wind away!"

But the fog rolled silently on, and before Sid knew what had happened he was completely surrounded by a dense, damp grayness. And the faster he flew, the thicker the fog grew, until he could barely see beyond his beak. Down, down he dived, hoping to land on solid ground.

All at once he found himself standing on top of a traffic-light signal right in the busiest part of town! Once inside the green "Go" signal, Sid began fluffing his wings, trying to dry them off before going on with his search for Midge.

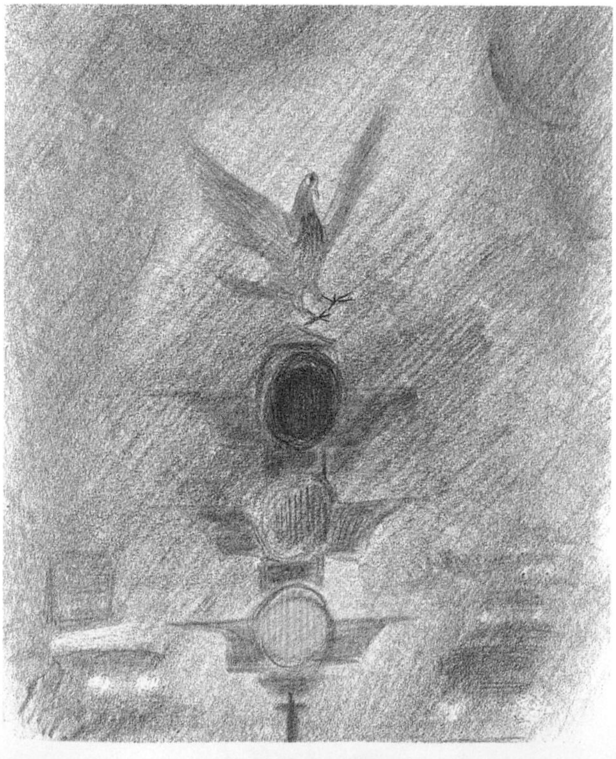

What Sid didn't know was that his fluffed up wings hid the word "Go," and no one in the street dared to budge. Soon there was a roar of automobile horns! "People certainly get awfully upset over a little fog!" said Sid as he stuck out his head.

Just then along came a policeman, and when he blew his whistle—BEEEP! BEEEP!—Sid flew out like a streak of lightning! At last the traffic could move on!

By now the fog had changed into rain and everybody started hopping aboard the cable cars—which is what people do in San Francisco wherever the hills are too steep or the weather is too wet.

And that's exactly what Sid did! Under the big bell on top of the cable car he found a perfect umbrella.

If only the conductor hadn't shouted "Hold on tight! Sharp corner ahead!" and then clanged the bell! The clapper of the bell hit Sid so hard that he fell overboard.

In the street gutter below, all bruised and weary, he hobbled along, muttering to himself, "People! It's all people's fault!"

But then he began to think of the kind man in the park. Would Mr. Hi Lee be there on such a terrible day as this? Sid tried to spread his wings and fly, but he was too weak. He would have to walk all the way to Union Square.

Fortunately the park was only a couple of blocks away, and just as Sid hopped up onto the curb he felt a gentle hand reach down and pick him up.

The next thing Sid knew he was inside Mr. Hi Lee's warm overcoat pocket, where, much to his surprise, he found several sunflower seeds. Right away he began to feel better. He could hardly wait to get on with his search for Midge.

When he peeped out, he saw that the rain had stopped and warm rays from the sun were beginning to shine down. Mr. Hi Lee talked to his friend inside his pocket as he walked along. "Around the corner from here I know of a bakery where we can get something more for you to eat," he said.

As they neared the shop Mr. Hi Lee noticed some men putting a large letter in the sign above the doorway. "Well, look at that—a new letter B!"

Out popped Sid's head, farther. What was that he heard? It sounded exactly like a certain bird he knew cooing. Could it be?

Yes indeed! It was his very own Midge! She had stayed with their nest through thick and thin.

Up flew Sid like an arrow shot from a bow. And oh, what a meeting! Such billing and cooing as you've never heard! And no wonder, for their two eggs were just about to hatch!

Out came two tiny beaks breaking through their shells!

And out of the bakery shop came the baker and his customers. They all wanted to know what the excitement was about.

Sid knew that his first duty was to find some food for Midge, so down he flew, and there was Mr. Hi Lee already holding out his hand full of cake crumbs!

After taking the crumbs to Midge, Sid hurried right back down, and this time he circled around and around Mr. Hi Lee's head flapping his wings happily. And we know what he meant by that!

Some time later, when their old neighbors came flying by, they saw Sid and Midge peacefully perched in the lower loop of the letter B and the two little ones in the upper loop. "Oh those lucky birds!" they cooed as they flew away. "Sid certainly did know what he was doing when he chose that letter B!"

MEET DON FREEMAN, AUTHOR AND ILLUSTRATOR

"All our ideas seem to come directly from experiences we have had. . . . For instance, the story for Fly High, Fly Low *stems from the experience we as a family have often had of living in a wonderful studio apartment only to have the building be removed from under us. . . . We once lived in Columbus Circle in New York but today if you were to try and find that apartment you would discover in its place the gigantic Coliseum!"*

URBAN ROOSTS

WHERE BIRDS NEST IN THE CITY

Barbara Bash

Early in the morning you can hear something rustling up on the ledge of an old stone building. Even before the city awakens, the birds are stirring in their urban roosts.

All across the country, as their natural habitats have been destroyed, birds have moved to town. The ones that have been able to adapt are thriving in the heart of the city.

One familiar urban dweller is the pigeon. Long ago it was called a rock dove, because it lived in the rocky cliffs along the coast of Europe. Today it flourishes all over the United States in the nooks and crannies of our cities.

To the pigeon, the city may look like a wilderness full of high cliffs and deep canyons. The cliffs are buildings made of stone and brick and glass, and the canyons are windy avenues full of cars and people. Flying together in flocks, pigeons explore the city canyons looking for food and spots to roost.

A roost is a place where birds go for protection when they sleep and for shelter from the rain and cold. Pigeons roost under highway overpasses, on window ledges, under building archways, on top of roofs, and under eaves. Sometimes their roosts are so well hidden you have to watch carefully to find them.

Look up under the train trestle. Pigeons may be roosting along the dark beams. Watch the open windows of an abandoned building. Hundreds of pigeons could be living inside, flying in and out all day long.

A nest is a place where birds lay their eggs and raise their chicks. Often it's in the same spot as the roost. Pigeons build a flimsy platform of sticks and twigs and debris up on a ledge, or on a windowsill, or in a flowerpot out on a fire escape, or in the curve of a storefront letter.

Throughout the year, pigeons lay eggs and hatch their young. The female sits quietly on her clutch, and after eighteen days, fuzzy chicks begin to appear. Five weeks later, after their adult feathers are fully developed, the young pigeons fly away to find homes of their own.

Sparrows and finches are successful city dwellers, too. Introduced from England in 1870 to control insects, the house sparrow has chosen to live close to people all across the United States. The house finch was originally a West Coast native, but some caged birds were released on the East Coast in 1940, and the species quickly spread. Sparrows and finches don't migrate, so you can watch them at backyard feeders throughout the year, chirping and chattering as they pick up seeds.

The little hollows in and around building ornaments and Gothic sculptures are favorite nesting spots for sparrows and finches. These cavity nesters can slip into the tiniest spaces. Some of their nests are visible and others are completely hidden from view.

In the spring, you may see a small bird flying overhead with a twig in its beak. If you follow its flight, it will lead you to its nest.

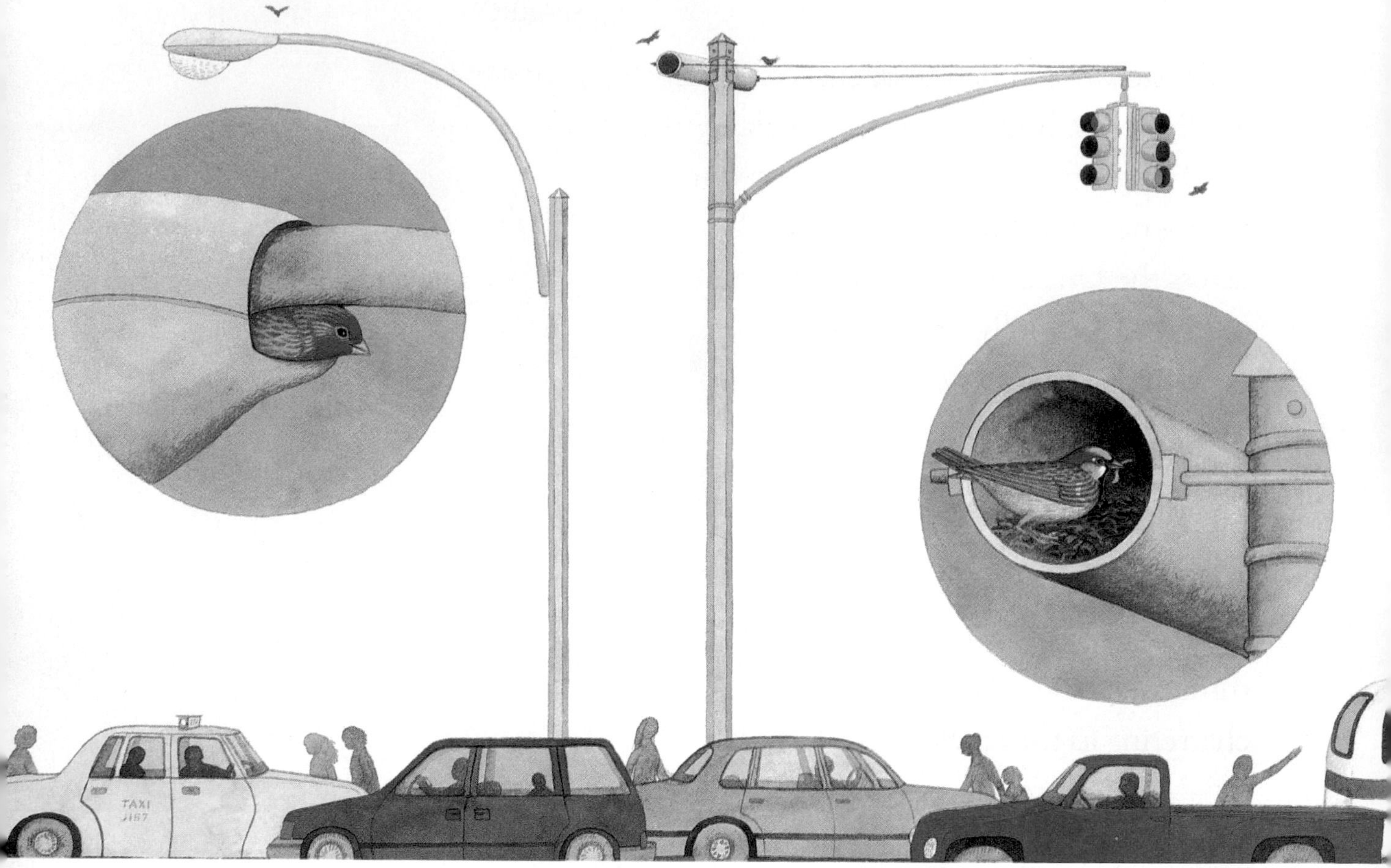

Watch the bird land and then disappear into a crevice or behind a stone curve. A few moments later it will pop out again, empty-beaked, and fly away to search for more nesting material.

Sparrows and finches can even find spots to nest out in the middle of the busiest intersections. At the top of some streetlights, there's a small opening where the lamp meets the pole. If you look carefully, you may see a tiny house finch slip inside.

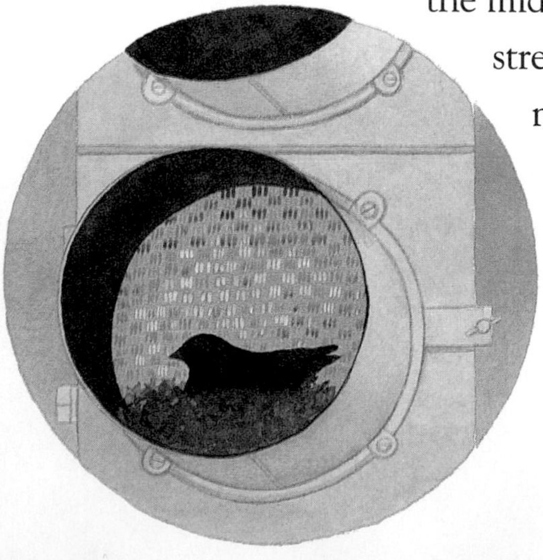

Or watch the short open pipe at the top of some traffic light poles. A pair of house sparrows may be darting in and out, bringing food to their nestlings. Sometimes you can even spot a nest in the metal casing that surrounds a traffic light. Perhaps the heat of the bulb keeps the eggs warm.

A tiled roof can house so many sparrows and finches it looks a little like an apartment complex. All day long the birds bring nesting material and food for their chicks into the small hidden cavities behind the tiles. When the chicks get too big for the nest, they play on top of the tiles, testing their wings before their first flight.

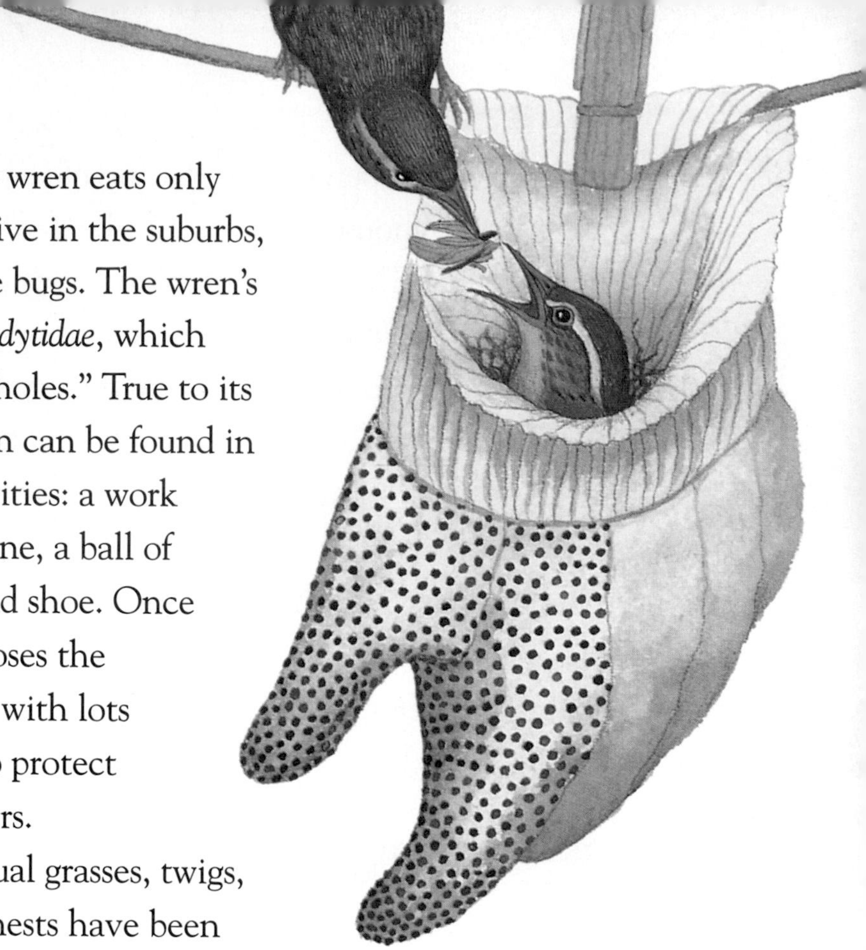

Because the house wren eats only insects, it prefers to live in the suburbs, where there are more bugs. The wren's family name is *Troglodytidae*, which means "creeper into holes." True to its name, the house wren can be found in the most unusual cavities: a work glove hanging on a line, a ball of twine, a teapot, an old shoe. Once the female wren chooses the cavity, she bolsters it with lots of nesting material to protect her eggs from intruders.

Along with the usual grasses, twigs, and feathers, wrens' nests have been found to contain hairpins, Kleenex, nails, wire, shoe buckles, candy wrappers, Band-Aids, paper clips, even dollar bills!

The barn owl lives in the city, too, but few people see it because it flies while everyone sleeps. All night long its pale, ghostly form soars over the buildings as it hunts for rats and mice to bring to its young.

The barn owl's eyes can see in the dark and its ears can hear the tiniest scratching. Even its voice is suited to city life. When it cries out in the night, it sounds like brakes screeching.

At daybreak, barn owls return to their nests to sleep. They like to live under train and highway overpasses and inside old barns and steeples. Instead of building nests, they lay their eggs in flat, protected spots.

As baby barn owls grow, they huddle together, hissing and slurping, as they wait for their parents to return with food.

The nighthawk is a ground-nesting bird: it looks for a level, open surface on which to lay its eggs. Because city ground is full of cars and people, the nighthawk often hatches its young up on flat graveled rooftops.

If you look up on a warm summer night, you might see a nighthawk swooping low over the street lights sweeping hundreds of insects into its large, gaping mouth. Or you might hear its call in the dark . . . *peent* . . .

Like the nighthawk, the killdeer makes no nest. It lays its eggs out in the open, in spots where the mottled eggshell pattern will be well camouflaged. In the city you might find killdeer eggs sitting on the gravel at the edge of a parking lot or next to a train track. Once, killdeer eggs were even found along the end line of a soccer field!

During the winter, crows flock together in large groups. They roost at night in the tops of trees in city parks. At dusk, one or two arrive first, perching on high branches and making a silky rustle with their wings. As the light fades, more crows appear and the clamor increases. They make rattling sounds, catlike cries, and metallic squeaks while they jostle for spots. As the darkness deepens, the calls gradually die down, until only an occasional gurgle is heard. Then the crows settle in for the night.

In November, snowy owls migrate down from the arctic tundra to spend the winter in northern cities. They seem to like the windswept environment of airport landing fields—perhaps because it reminds them of home. The owls roost out on the open ground, blending in with the snowy whiteness.

At dusk the snowy owls begin hunting for mice, rats, and rabbits. They fly slowly and silently, their heads turning from side to side, their eyes scanning the ground for movement. Sometimes snowy owls will crouch on a small mound of snow and wait, completely still, for prey to wander by. The sound of the jets doesn't seem to faze them at all.

Cars and trucks lumber noisily over big city bridges. But underneath, hidden among the beams and girders, peregrine falcons have found a home. Sleekly built with powerful wings, the falcon is one of the fastest birds on earth. In the city it soars high above the bridges and buildings, hunting for pigeons and small birds flying below. When it spots its prey, the falcon folds its wings tight against its body and dives straight down at speeds of over one hundred fifty miles per hour!

In cities all across the country, people are fascinated with the peregrine falcon and are doing what they can to make this noble bird feel welcome. In many cities people set nesting boxes filled with gravel out on skyscraper ledges. The falcons seem to like these windy, rocky heights, for they return to the boxes early each spring to lay their eggs and raise their chicks. Living on these high perches with no natural enemies and plenty of pigeons, the falcons are adapting well to urban life.

So many birds make their homes in the midst of the city—sparrows and finches, barn owls and snowy owls, nighthawks and killdeers, pigeons and wrens, crows, and falcons. Each has found its own urban roost.

THE WORM

Raymond Souster

Don't ask me how he managed
to corkscrew his way
through the King Street Pavement,
I'll leave that to you.

All I know is
there he was,
circling, uncoiling
his shining three inches,
wiggling all ten toes
as the warm rain fell
in that dark morning street
of early April.

illustrated by Robert Byrd

PIGEONS

Lilian Moore

Pigeons are city folk
content
to live with concrete
and cement.

They seldom
try
the sky.

A pigeon never sings
of hill
and flowering hedge,
but busily commutes
from sidewalk
to his ledge.

Oh pigeon, what a waste of wings!

MAKE WAY FOR DUCKLINGS

Robert McCloskey

Mr. and Mrs. Mallard were looking for a place to live. But every time Mr. Mallard saw what looked like a nice place, Mrs. Mallard said it was no good. There were sure to be foxes in the woods or turtles in the water, and she was not going to raise a family where there might be foxes or turtles. So they flew on and on.

When they got to Boston, they felt too tired to fly any further. There was a nice pond in the Public Garden, with a little island on it. "The very place to spend the night," quacked Mr. Mallard. So down they flapped.

Next morning they fished for their breakfast in the mud at the bottom of the pond. But they didn't find much.

Just as they were getting ready to start on their way, a strange enormous bird came by. It was pushing a boat full of people, and there was a man sitting on its back. "Good morning," quacked Mr. Mallard, being polite. The big bird was too proud to answer. But the people on the boat threw peanuts into the water, so the Mallards followed them all round the pond and got another breakfast, better than the first.

"I like this place," said Mrs. Mallard as they climbed out on the bank and waddled along. "Why don't we build a nest and raise our ducklings right in this pond? There are no foxes and no turtles, and the people feed us peanuts. What could be better?"

"Good," said Mr. Mallard, delighted that at last Mrs. Mallard had found a place that suited her. But—

"Look out!" squawked Mrs. Mallard, all of a dither. "You'll get run over!" And when she got her breath she added: "*This* is no place for babies, with all those horrid things rushing about. We'll have to look somewhere else."

So they flew over Beacon Hill and round the State House, but there was no place there.

They looked in Louisburg Square, but there was no water to swim in.

Then they flew over the Charles River. "This is better," quacked Mr. Mallard. "That island looks like a nice quiet place, and it's only a little way from the Public Garden."

"Yes," said Mrs. Mallard, remembering the peanuts. "That looks like just the right place to hatch ducklings."

So they chose a cozy spot among the bushes near the water and settled down to build their nest. And only just in time, for now they were beginning to molt. All their old wing feathers started to drop out, and they would not be able to fly again until the new ones grew in.

But of course they could swim, and one day they swam over to the park on the river bank, and there they met a policeman called Michael. Michael fed them peanuts, and after that the Mallards called on Michael every day.

After Mrs. Mallard had laid eight eggs in the nest she couldn't go to visit Michael any more, because she had to sit on the eggs to keep them warm. She moved off the nest only to get a drink of water, or to have her lunch, or to count the eggs and make sure they were all there.

One day the ducklings hatched out. First came Jack, then Kack, and then Lack, then Mack and Nack and Ouack and Pack and Quack. Mr. and Mrs. Mallard were bursting with pride. It was a great responsibility taking care of so many ducklings, and it kept them very busy.

One day Mr. Mallard decided he'd like to take a trip to see what the rest of the river was like, further on. So off he set. "I'll meet you in a week, in the Public Garden," he quacked over his shoulder. "Take good care of the ducklings."

"Don't you worry," said Mrs. Mallard. "I know all about bringing up children." And she did.

She taught them how to swim and dive.

She taught them to walk in a line, to come when they were called, and to keep a safe distance from bikes and scooters and other things with wheels.

When at last she felt perfectly satisfied with them, she said one morning: "Come along, children. Follow me." Before you could wink an eyelash Jack, Kack, Lack, Mack, Nack, Ouack, Pack, and Quack fell into line, just as they had been taught. Mrs. Mallard led the way into the water and they swam behind her to the opposite bank.

There they waded ashore and waddled along till they came to the highway.

Mrs. Mallard stepped out to cross the road. "Honk, honk!" went the horns on the speeding cars. "Qua-a-ack!" went Mrs. Mallard as she tumbled back again. "Quack! Quack! Quack! Quack!" went Jack, Kack, Lack, Mack, Nack, Ouack, Pack, and Quack, just as loud as their little quackers could quack. The cars kept speeding by and honking, and Mrs. Mallard and the ducklings kept right on quack-quack-quacking.

They made such a noise that Michael came running, waving his arms and blowing his whistle.

He planted himself in the center of the road, raised one hand to stop the traffic, and then beckoned with the other, the way policemen do, for Mrs. Mallard to cross over.

As soon as Mrs. Mallard and the ducklings were safe on the other side and on their way down Mount Vernon Street, Michael rushed back to his police booth.

He called Clancy at headquarters and said: "There's a family of ducks walkin' down the street!" Clancy said: "Family of *what?*" "*Ducks!*" yelled Michael. "Send a police car, quick!"

Meanwhile Mrs. Mallard had reached the Corner Book Shop and turned into Charles Street, with Jack, Kack, Lack, Mack, Nack, Ouack, Pack, and Quack all marching in line behind her.

Everyone stared. An old lady from Beacon Hill said: "Isn't it amazing!" and the man who swept the streets said: "Well, now, ain't that nice!" and when Mrs. Mallard heard them she was so proud she tipped her nose in the air and walked along with an extra swing in her waddle.

When they came to the corner of Beacon Street there was the police car with four policemen that Clancy had

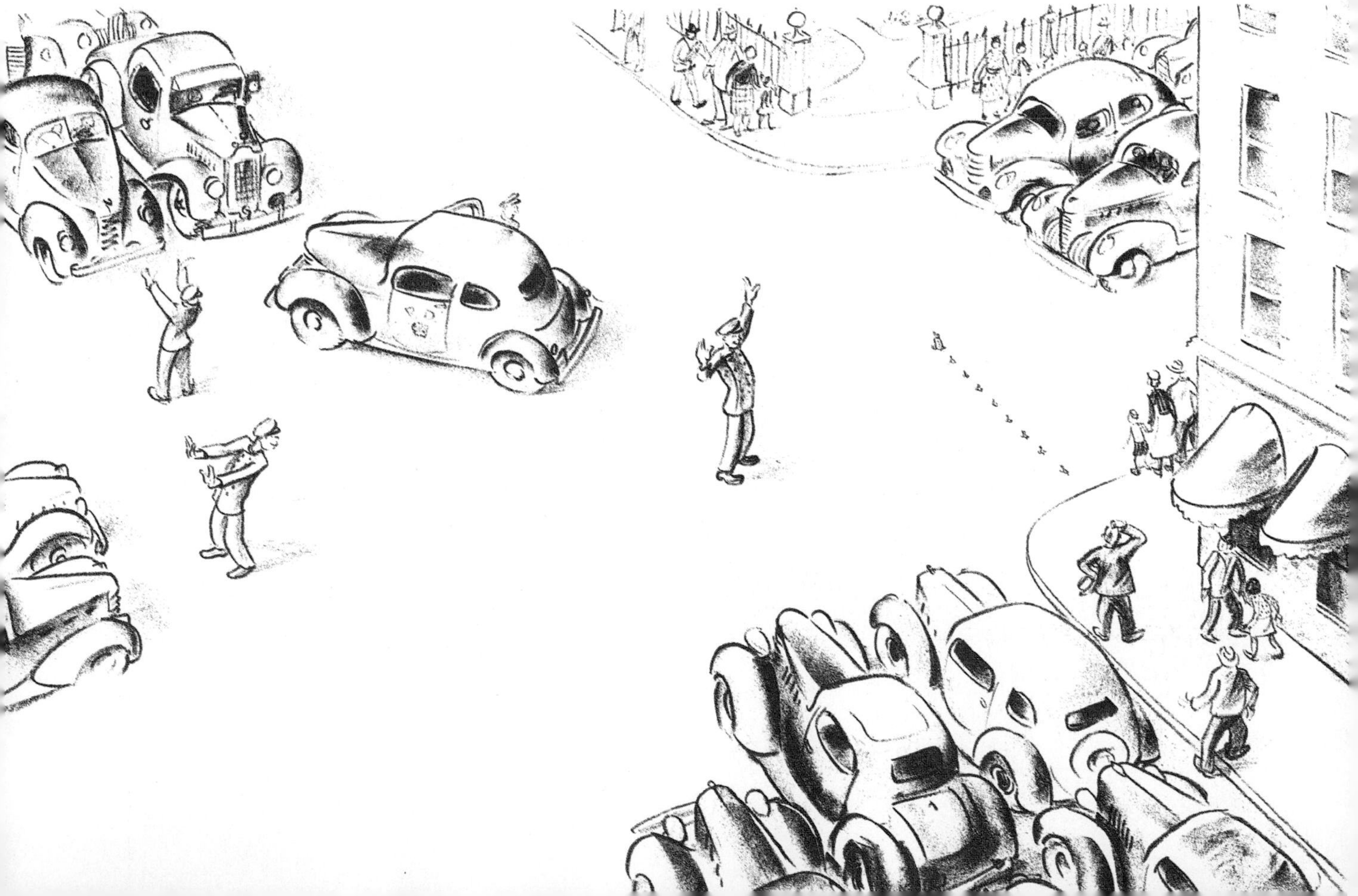

sent from headquarters. The policemen held back the traffic so Mrs. Mallard and the ducklings could march across the street, right on into the Public Garden.

Inside the gate they all turned round to say thank you to the policemen. The policemen smiled and waved good-by.

When they reached the pond and swam across to the little island, there was Mr. Mallard waiting for them, just as he had promised.

The ducklings liked the new island so much that they decided to live there. All day long they follow the swan boats and eat peanuts.

And when night falls they swim to their little island and go to sleep.

MEET ROBERT McCLOSKEY, AUTHOR AND ILLUSTRATOR

Robert McCloskey studied ducks for a long time before he drew the illustrations for Make Way for Ducklings. *He went to the Natural History Museum in New York where he took careful notice of stuffed mallards. He talked to people who knew all about ducks. But he felt he needed live models so he bought four mallard ducks from a city poultry dealer. "I spent the next weeks on my hands and knees, armed with a box of Kleenex and a sketch book, following ducks around the studio and observing them in the bathtub,"* McCloskey *said. "No effort is too great to find out as much as possible about the things you are drawing. It's a good feeling to be able to put down a line and know that it is right."*

FINE ART
CITY WILDLIFE

Boston Common at Twilight. 1885–86. Frederick Childe Hassam.

Oil on canvas. Gift of Miss Maud E. Appleton, Museum of Fine Arts, Boston

Lunch in the Gardens. 1985. Beryl Cook.

Oil on masonite. From *Beryl Cook's New York*, John Murray Publishing. © 1985 Beryl Cook.
Reproduced by arrangement with Rogers, Coleridge & White Ltd.
Photo: Flannagan Graphics, New Jersey

CITY SUPERHEROES

from The City Kid's Field Guide
by Ethan Herberman

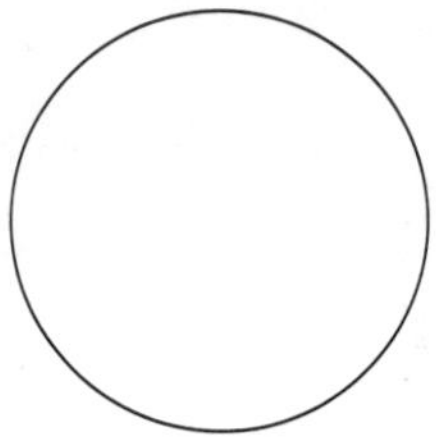

AND NOW A WORD ABOUT RATS

Do you see this circle? It's just wide enough for a rat to crawl through.

Have you touched a cement block? It's just soft enough for a rat to chew.

Have you seen the world's fastest man on television? He moves about as fast as the world's most ordinary rat.

Start collecting facts like these and you soon understand why a famous zoologist called rats "the finest . . . product that Nature has managed to create on this planet." Without question, they stand out among city creatures, mainly by not standing out at all. You can spend hours watching pigeons, but unless you are unusually observant, you may never encounter the rats.

Fat, fat, the water rat! About eight inches long from nose to tail and well-fed, this brown rat (also known as a Norway, water, or sewer rat) belongs to the species most often found in the U.S. But you might also see smaller, black (or roof) rats, usually in high places, when the larger species hasn't driven them away.

But that doesn't mean they live someplace else. In big cities they live *everywhere*—in subways, attics, basements and backyards, inside sewer pipes, and underneath wharves. They pop up in people's toilets; they scurry in the shadows of fancy restaurants, sharing dinner with the guests. They live up to their reputation as destroyers of property, spreaders of disease—and the animal superheroes of city life.

They seem to have learned every survival trick in town. Does it help to be "nocturnal"—to be active at night? Well, rats are nocturnal. With their sensitive whiskers they find their way expertly in the lightless spaces between walls. Does it help to be "omnivorous"—to eat a lot of different foods? Well, rats are omnivorous. With teeth that grow nonstop, they gnaw away at everything from grain to pigeons to other rats. Does it help to reproduce quickly? Well, a single female, breeding seven times a year, could theoretically produce 168 new rats during a typical two-year lifespan. Above all, though, these rodents are smart. Consider the brown rat, for instance,

by far the most successful of the two rat species among us. Brown rats have learned a lot since spreading out across the world from their Asian burrows. In the old days, they would swallow almost anything that smelled good. But try poisoning brown rats now. They will barely sample unfamiliar food. And even if you did succeed in hurting one, bad news travels fast! A special chemical called a "distress pheromone" would spread from rat to rat in the victim's tribe, and nobody in that tightly knit family of ten to two hundred members would ever touch your bait again.

So how do we get rid of them—with special poisons expertly applied? That sometimes works, but for long term solutions, most health officials say, "build them out" and "starve them out": clean up slums, seal up buildings, put food out of reach. That may seem impossible; but perhaps we had better try, for by now there may be one rat for every two people in the United States. And all together, they destroy about one billion dollars worth of food and property every year.

"But that's impossible," you might say as you pick up the trash strewn all over the yard. "I sealed those cans firmly last night."

Any number of night roamers might have done it: skunks, squirrels, dogs, even your neighbor's cat. But if you really pressed those lids down tight, latched the box, even weighed it down with a heavy rock, then the chances are that the mess was caused by a raccoon.

And chances are it'll be back to do it again tonight.

People seem to have tried everything in their war with these large-brained animals. They've latched chicken coops, and the raccoons unlatched them; they've sealed up

Every can is a treasure. A mother raccoon and her cubs dig into someone's garbage. Notice their furry "masks," powerful bodies, and banded tails. About the only items they won't eat are raw onions.

©Steve Maslowski/Photo Researchers

doorways, and the raccoons came in through the chimney; they've hung sacks of bird food on strings from trees, and the raccoons untied—didn't chew through, *untied*—the string.

Despite efforts to deter them, raccoon numbers are booming: More of them wander through some North American communities than ever prowled the same regions before the cities were built. One study turned up 150 per square mile in an Ohio suburb. They're fat, too, as you have probably seen.

To understand the raccoon's success, follow the next one you see waddling through mud or snow. Don't come too near—don't ever approach or corner a raccoon because it may carry rabies and may bite you. Instead, examine the tracks it leaves behind. Don't the forepaws look like a small child's hands? They are about that sensitive, and what's more, the raccoon is ready to take full advantage of whatever gets within its grasp.

It eats just about everything that comes its way—everything meaning berries, frogs, fish, beetles, breakfast cereal, even kittens. Like the cockroach, it has adapted well to the buildings of humans. In the wild, raccoon nests are often found in hollow trees; but in the city they have been found in sewers, culverts, garages and attics, not to mention the ventilation systems of buildings downtown.

How do raccoons pry off lids and untie string? With sensitive front paws that look much like a child's hands and leave similar imprints in mud and snow.

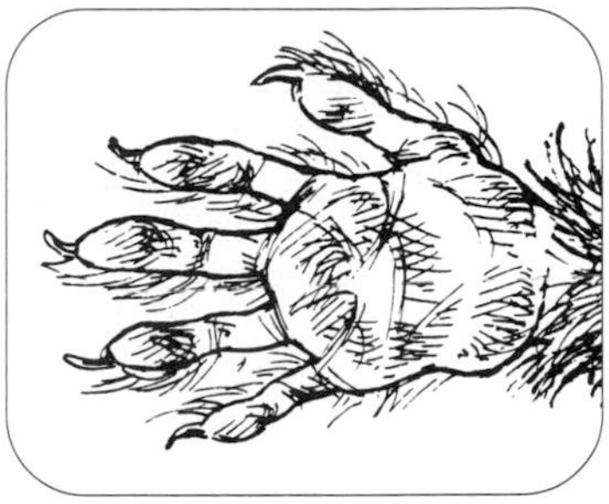

raccoon's forepaw

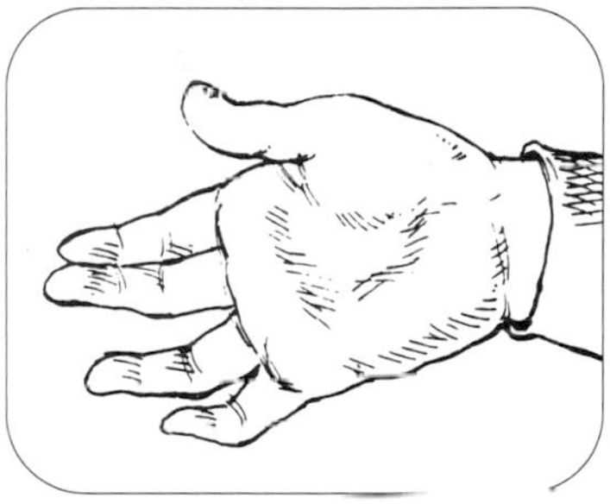

child's hand

RACCOON

Mary Ann Hoberman
illustrated by Pamela Carroll

Crash goes the trashcan! Clatter and clacket!
What in the world can be making that racket?
I hurry to look by the light of the moon.
And what do I find? Why, a fine fat raccoon!
All through the garden the garbage he's strewn,
And he's eating his supper, that robber raccoon,
Eating so nicely without fork or spoon,
Why, his manners are perfect, that thieving raccoon!
And wasn't he smart to discover that pail?
And wasn't he smart to uncover that pail?
And isn't he lucky he won't go to jail
For stealing his dinner and making a mess
For me to clean up in the morning, I guess,
While he, the old pirate, abundantly fed,
Curls up in a ball fast asleep in his bed.

MEET MARY ANN HOBERMAN, POET

"We had a swing in our backyard and I would swing back and forth, up and down, for hours at a time, making up songs that I sang to myself. It was the rhythm of the swinging that got me started and gave me my ideas and put the tunes in my head. As I swung higher and higher and faster and faster, I would sing louder and louder until I was shouting my songs out at the top of my voice and my mother would come out to see what was happening. Then I would let the swing slow down and the rhythm would get slower and my song would get softer and more dreamy and the afternoon would drift away."

©Richard Kolar/Animals Animals

CITY CRITTERS

Richard Chevat

The city. Tall buildings. Shoppers with their arms full of packages. People hurrying along. Buses, cabs, cars—and wild animals.

Wild animals? You bet. Cities and towns are filled with wildlife.

"When most people think of wildlife, they think of grizzly bears or elk or white-tailed deer. But *all* the wild animals that live in a city are wildlife, including butterflies, ants, pigeons and even rats," says Mike Matthews. He's a

These city ducks might cause a traffic jam.

©Charles Palek/Animals Animals

scientist who works for New York state, trying to protect its wildlife, both in the woods and in the cities.

Why does a rat deserve to be called "wildlife"? Charles Nilon, a biologist for the Kansas Department of Wildlife and Parks explains: "Any animal that you see that is not a pet, that doesn't depend on people taking care of it, is a wild animal."

SKYSCRAPER GEESE, PARK RACCOONS

On the tenth floor of an office building in St. Louis, Missouri, is a nest of Canadian geese. They've been spending summers there for the past six years.

Dave Tylka is an urban biologist—a scientist who studies wildlife in cities. He talked about the skyscraper geese. "There's a type of Canadian geese that nest on cliffs over the Mississippi River," he said. "These particular geese must have thought that a balcony looked like a good cliff to nest on!"

If geese on an office building sound strange, how about raccoons in the heart of New York City? Mike Matthews says they live in sewers, in buildings, and especially in New York's Central Park. "People think that animals want to be near trees or open spaces. But raccoons will live in chimneys and sewers."

Raccoons live in sewers and parks.
They find food in garbage cans.
©Ted Levin/Animals Animals

BIRD'S-EYE VIEW

According to Matthews, city parks are great places to go bird-watching, especially in the early spring and fall. "They're like islands of green space where migrating birds will stop," he says.

A streetlight makes a good perch for this eagle.

When Mike Matthews talks about birds, he doesn't just mean "city birds" like sparrows, starlings and pigeons. "There's much, much more," he says. "In the city limits, there are great blue herons, owls and all sorts of water birds. Even a bald eagle will visit from time to time."

You might think these creatures would try to avoid cities. Not so, says Matthews. Animals will live wherever they can find food, shelter and a place to raise their young.

SCIENTISTS' HELPERS

Scientists can learn a lot about a city by studying the wild animals that live there. "If you're concerned about pollution or waste, looking at wildlife is one way to learn about it," says Charles Nilon, the Kansas biologist.

"For example, in Florida, scientists studied squirrels that lived by highways. The scientists wanted to find out how the squirrels had been affected by breathing car exhaust. Because they breathe the fumes all day, any health

Squirrels and chipmunks are common wildlife in cities. This chipmunk is stealing some birdseed from a window ledge.

problems will show up in squirrels before they show up in humans."

Sometimes, very rare animals can survive well in cities. Take the peregrine falcon. This bird had almost disappeared in the eastern United States. About 15 years ago, scientists began trying to save the peregrine falcon by raising baby falcons in laboratories and releasing them in the wild.

Today, the bird is making a comeback, and several falcons have come back to nest in the middle of big cities. There, they've found just the right kinds of shelter and food. They rest on skyscraper "cliffs," and they hunt city birds—pigeons and starlings.

Not all animals find city homes as easily as falcons have. That's why scientists create and protect special animal habitats—spots with the right amounts of water and food and the kinds of trees and plants an animal needs to survive.

At the Gateway National Recreation Area in New York City, scientists have set aside a small "grasslands" habitat—a flat, open field. Don Reipe, a scientist at Gateway, explained why: "Grasslands are vanishing because they're used for homes, shopping malls and other developments. But it's an important habitat for animals like the upland sandpiper, the meadowlark and the short-eared owl. Our grasslands area is a home to all these birds."

Scientists in Des Moines, Iowa, built a different kind of habitat—a garden that grows goodies for butterflies. It's in the state fairgrounds. "We planted a garden designed to attract 40 different species of butterflies," says Laura Jackson, an Iowa biologist. "The idea is to show people how they can attract butterflies to their backyards by planting the right flowers and plants."

©Richard Shiell/Animals Animals

Most people don't see the wild animals all around them—because they don't know what to look for. Stephen Petland, a biologist in Seattle, Washington, says careful observation—and a look at a few bird and animal guides—can make the difference.

"In one neighborhood in Seattle, over the course of a year, I might be able to find 40 or 50 different types of birds," notes Petland.

You don't have to be a scientist to study wildlife in cities or towns. Just keep an eagle eye when you're playing in your yard, your playground or your neighborhood park. And when you're walking down the street, don't forget: Watch out for wild animals!

Deer are moving closer to cities. Some have been spotted in city parks.

©Wendy Shatil & Bob Rozinski/Tom Stack & Associates

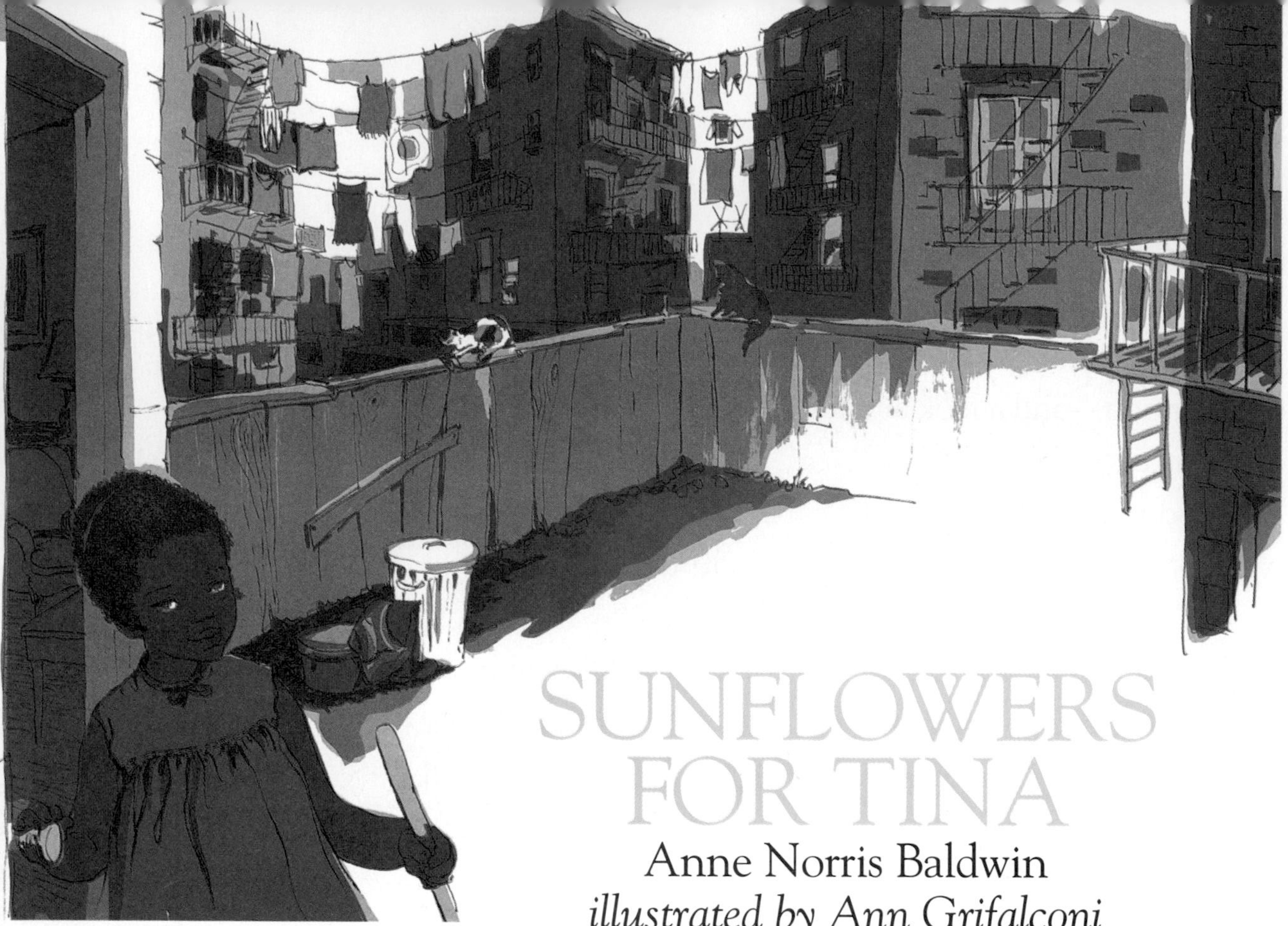

SUNFLOWERS FOR TINA

Anne Norris Baldwin

illustrated by Ann Grifalconi

Tina wanted to grow something. The back yard had a square of dirt that might have been a garden. Nothing grew because no one had planted anything. Behind the square of dirt was a board fence that had once been painted green, and behind that was an alley.

Overhead, the laundry flapped, and sometimes a cat walked the fence, and sometimes Tina's mother leaned out of a window to talk to a neighbor in another window.

Sometimes her brother Eddie drummed on the lid of the garbage can till Tina was ready to scream, and sometimes he didn't because the lid got too hot in summer. Then he and the other boys would turn on the fire hydrant and splash quickly through the cold torrent to cool off before the cops got there.

Tina asked her mother if they could have a garden.

Her mother said, "No. Where'd we have a garden? A garden's a luxury. We're not rich, you know."

"Out back," said Tina, "we could have a garden. There's dirt."

"You just try and grow something in New York City dirt," said Tina's mother.

A block away, Mr. Samuels had his newsstand. He sold cigarettes and candy too, and sometimes he had a few bunches of flowers stuck in a pail of water.

Tina asked Mr. Samuels where he got his flowers.

"From a florist," he said. "I don't sell enough to get 'em from a wholesaler."

"Where do flowers grow?" Tina asked.

"Lord, I don't know. In the country somewheres. In a greenhouse, maybe."

"Don't any grow in New York?"

"I don't think so. I can't think where they would."

Tina had a nickel tied in a handkerchief.

"What will a nickel buy?"

"Lifesavers or gum. Most things are ten. 'Less you want to read the news."

"No."

"Lifesavers or gum then."

Tina bought cherry lifesavers. When she stuck her tongue out, she could see the lifesaver on it.

Outside his grocery store, Mr. Jones was winding an awning down to keep the sun off the vegetables. The lettuce already looked wilted, but the carrots and onions and radishes were fat and bright as robins.

Tina wanted to ask Mr. Jones if vegetables grew in New York, but he didn't seem to have noticed her standing there. He shook some water over the vegetables and went back inside.

The house sounded very quiet when Tina got home. Her mother was out at work. The upstairs kids weren't there. Eddie wasn't even banging around in the back room. Tina's grandmother sat in her corner of the bedroom, but she never made any noise. She was like a charred old stump, dark and gnarled and bent forever in the same position. Tina wished that she would only say something sometimes. Then Tina would be sure that her grandmother was really alive.

It was going to be a hot day. The kitchen smelled musty. The laundry strung between their building and the next one hung limply. Nothing moved.

Tina looked in the refrigerator. She drank a cool glass of milk and put the carton back on its shelf. It was then that she noticed the bunch of bulging carrots, with tops as fresh and ruffled as Tina's Easter dress. Lush and bounteous gardens sprang into her mind. Acres and acres of greenery grew before her very eyes.

Very quickly and eagerly, Tina untwisted the wire that held the carrots together. She took out half the bunch, and then she put the wire back around the others and replaced them carefully at just their original angle. As she closed the refrigerator door, the hot air from outside rushed back against her face.

Tina took the carrots and a dirty spoon from the sink and went outside. She knelt down on the cracked concrete in front of the little square of earth by the fence, not even noticing that she scraped her knee. The ground was dry and hard. Tina dug at it with the spoon, but she couldn't make much of a hole. The handle of the spoon bent, and she hurt her hand trying to straighten it out.

Tina went inside for some water. The faucet wouldn't stop dripping after she had filled a glass; she gave up and let it drip. She poured the water into the ground where she had been digging and went back for more. The water made digging a little easier. Finally, she was able to bury a stubby carrot altogether.

At last, Tina had planted four carrots in a neat row in front of the fence. The green feathery tops stuck up

cheerfully in the sun. She watered them with great and affectionate care.

Tina rinsed the dirt off the spoon and left it in the sink where she had found it. She heard her grandmother moving clumsily in the bedroom, and went to the door. It took a moment for her eyes to get used to the dim light.

"Would you like a drink of water?" she asked her grandmother. It was all she could think of. She considered telling her about the garden, but it didn't seem worthwhile: her grandmother never answered her.

The old lady nodded silently, and Tina brought her a glass. Tina sat down on the floor at her feet. She dug the lifesavers out of her dress pocket, and peeled one off for her grandmother, whose hand shook a little as she took it.

Tina waited impatiently for her mother to come home. From time to time, she went out back and looked at her garden. The day dragged slowly on. The carrot tops began to droop in the hot sun.

From the next yard came the sound of Eddie practicing a tune on his harmonica. Tina hoped that he wouldn't see her garden before their mother did. She was sure Eddie would laugh.

Finally, the gate clicked, and Tina began sweeping the kitchen so that her mother wouldn't see her excitement.

Tina's mother came heavily through the back door and began putting away a bag of groceries. Then she washed her hot face at the sink and changed into her slippers. "Phew," she said, wringing her hands. "Summer's here."

Tina danced in a circle around her broom. She did a low curtsy to her mother for fun.

"What's with you, child?"

"Oh nothing. Didn't you notice anything?"

Tina's mother looked all around the room. Then she looked at Tina with a puzzled expression. Tina laughed.

"Give up?"

"Give up."

"My garden!"

Tina swished past her mother and out the door before her mother had time to be surprised. She planted herself proudly in front of the little row of drooping carrot tops and spread out her arms happily toward the sun.

Tina's mother stood squarely in the doorway, her hands on her hips. She stared at Tina.

"What on earth . . .?"

"I planted it myself," said Tina proudly.

"You didn't—!"

"Carrots," explained Tina. "They should grow." But her voice sounded uncertain by the end of the sentence.

"Oh no," said Tina's mother with a look of dismay. "Not our supper. You just dig those right up again!"

The summer went right on being hot and heavy. Even the pigeons looked hot. They waddled lazily around the flat rooftops. Tina's mother swore when they got the laundry dirty.

Eddie got a shoeshine kit from his uncle and spent most of his time hanging around downtown where business was better.

"Why can't you find something to do?" Eddie asked Tina. "Anything's better than just sitting around."

"Like what?"

"I don't know. Help Mom."

"I do."

"You don't."

When Tina started to cry, Eddie felt sorry and said, "Well, don't feel bad. Shinin' shoes ain't no fun either."

"I wish we had a garden." Tina said. She hadn't meant to tell Eddie, but it just came out.

"A garden?" Eddie repeated. "What for?"

"Just to look at. It'd be pretty."

Eddie sat down on the kitchen step. He put the garbage can between his knees and began to drum. He looked thoughtful. Then he said, "I'll be back," and swung through the rickety gate. She could hear him whistling as he loped down the alley.

Later, he came back and said, "I'll show you a garden, Sis," and he jerked his head toward the street.

Tina followed him some three blocks. She felt warmly happy.

Eddie stopped at the edge of an empty lot. "There," he said. "Sunflowers!"

Above them, the side wall of the first building bore the imprint of old walls and chimneys, as if a house had been turned inside out. Once there had been a building instead of the empty lot, and people had lived in it. Now, nothing was left except some broken bricks and crumbled mortar, and the black outline of rooms against the next wall.

Out of the rubble of brick and old cement, two stalks, taller than Tina herself, rose toward the sky. Each one lifted a yellow sun to light the day.

"How beautiful," said Tina. The harsh ruins of the broken building made them seem remarkable. It didn't matter that they weren't her own; they were there for anyone to see.

Eddie started forward to pick them for her.

"No, don't," Tina said.

He hesitated, trying for a moment to understand the expression on her face. Then he shrugged. She heard his penknife click shut inside his hand.

Tina was thinking of something quite different. She had suddenly remembered her old grandmother, hunched and silent in her dark corner, with only the whites of her eyes seeming to move. Her life was dark and old and crumbled, like the empty lot. Tina could only guess what it once had been. There didn't seem to be any sunflowers—any bright spots at all—left in her grandmother's life.

At home, Tina put on her yellow dress. It was almost too small for her, but the color was bright and beautiful against her dark skin.

Around the bedroom she danced. As she twirled, her full skirt filled with air and stood out from her waist, a golden disk of petals.

Tina could feel her grandmother's eyes follow her around the room questioningly.

"I'm a sunflower," Tina said.

Even though the room was very dark, Tina could see her grandmother's whole face crinkle into a smile. The whites of her eyes shone, and her thin shoulders shook under her shawl. Out of the cave between her cheeks came a distant rumble of laughter which Tina had never heard before.

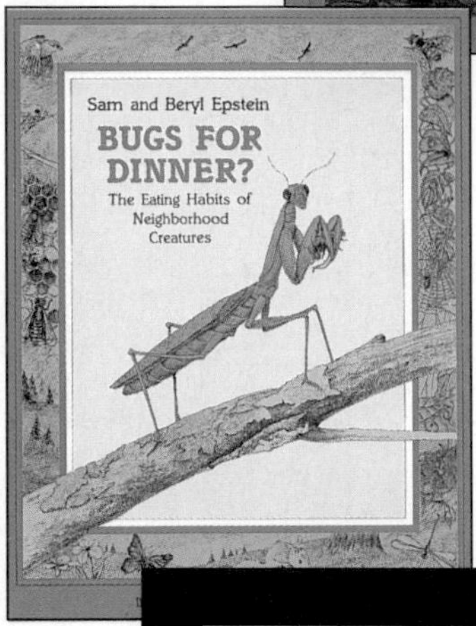

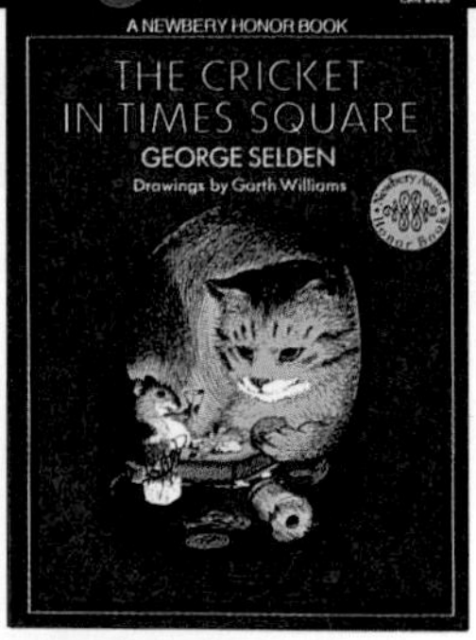

BIBLIOGRAPHY

Animals in Cities and Parks by Raintree Publishers. This book is chock-full of information about squirrels, birds, insects, and other animals that share their living space with people.

Bugs for Dinner? The Eating Habits of Neighborhood Creatures by Sam and Beryl Epstein. Did you ever wonder how squirrels, birds, insects, and other small city creatures find food and avoid being eaten themselves? This book will help you find out.

City Geese by Ron Hirschi. Canada Geese are becoming more and more a part of city life. The author follows a colony of geese in Fort Collins, Colorado, through one year of their life.

The Cricket in Times Square by George Selden. You'll enjoy reading this classic tale about the adventures of a cricket from Connecticut who spends a summer in a New York City subway.

The Empty Lot by Dale H. Fife. Harry, who is about to sell an unwanted empty lot, discovers after close inspection that it's not empty at all.

Exploring Spring by Sandra Markle. Have some fun with this collection of springtime activities including stories, puzzles, and observations of wildlife.

Greening the City Streets: The Story of Community Gardens by Barbara A. Huff. Take a tour of a community garden in New York City and learn how all the neighborhood residents helped make it.

Squirrel Watching by Miriam Schlein. In the city, squirrels are easy to find and fun to watch. This book tells all about squirrel behavior—how they gather food, build their nests, and raise their young.

STORYTELLING

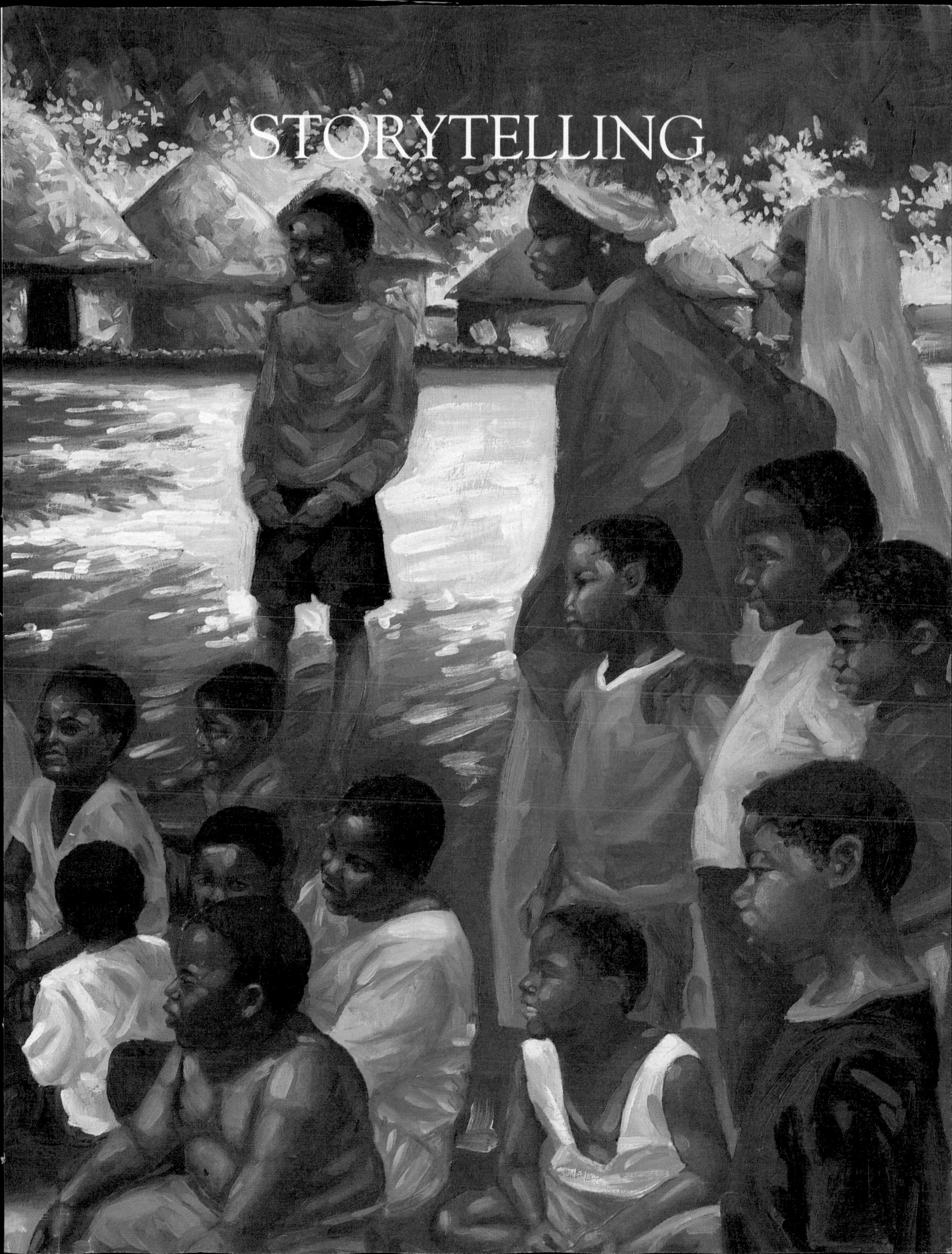

A STORY, A STORY

retold and illustrated by Gail E. Haley

Most African stories, whether or not they are about Kwaku Ananse the "spider man," are called "Spider Stories." This book is about how that came to be.

"Spider stories" tell how small, defenseless men or animals outwit others and succeed against great odds. These stories crossed the Atlantic Ocean in the cruel ships that delivered slaves to the Americas. Their descendants still tell some of these stories today. Ananse has become Anancy in the Caribbean isles, while he survives as "Aunt Nancy" in the southern United States.

You will find many African words in this story. If you listen carefully, you can tell what they mean by their sounds. At times words and phrases are repeated several times. Africans repeat words to make them stronger. For example: "So small, so small, so small," means very, very, very small.

This story begins as do all African stories: "We do not really mean, we do not really mean that what we are about to say is true. A story, a story; let it come, let it go."

Once, oh small children round my knee, there were no stories on earth to hear. All the stories belonged to Nyame, the Sky God. He kept them in a golden box next to his royal stool.

Ananse, the Spider man, wanted to buy the Sky God's stories. So he spun a web up to the sky.

When the Sky God heard what Ananse wanted, he laughed: "Twe, twe, twe. The price of my stories is that you bring me Osebo the leopard of-the-terrible-teeth, Mmboro the hornet who-stings-like-fire, and Mmoatia the fairy whom-men-never-see."

Ananse bowed and answered: "I shall gladly pay the price."

"Twe, twe, twe," chuckled the Sky God. "How can a weak old man like you, so small, so small, so small pay my price?"

But Ananse merely climbed down to earth to find the things that the Sky God demanded.

Ananse ran along the jungle path—yiridi, yiridi, yiridi—till he came to Osebo the leopard-of-the-terrible-teeth.

"Oho, Ananse," said the leopard, "you are just in time to be my lunch."

Ananse replied: "As for that, what will happen will happen. But first let us play the binding binding game."

The leopard, who was fond of games, asked: "How is it played?"

"With vine creepers," explained Ananse. "I will bind you by your foot and foot. Then I will untie you, and you can tie me up."

"Very well," growled the leopard, who planned to eat Ananse as soon as it was his turn to bind him.

So Ananse tied the leopard by his foot, by his foot, by his foot, by his foot, with the vine creeper. Then he said: "Now, Osebo, you are ready to meet the Sky God." And he hung the tied leopard in a tree in the jungle.

Next Ananse cut a frond from a banana tree and filled a calabash with water. He crept through the tall grasses, sora, sora, sora, till he came to the nest of Mmboro, the hornets-who-sting-like-fire.

Ananse held the banana leaf over his head as an umbrella. Then he poured some of the water in the calabash over his head.

The rest he emptied over the hornet's nest and cried: "It is raining, raining, raining. Should you not fly into my calabash, so that the rain will not tatter your wings?"

"Thank you. Thank you," hummed the hornets, and they flew into the calabash—fom! Ananse quickly stopped the mouth of the gourd.

"Now, Mmbora, you are ready to meet the Sky God," said Ananse. And he hung the calabash full of hornets onto the tree next to the leopard.

Ananse now carved a little wooden doll holding a bowl. He covered the doll from top to bottom with sticky latex gum. Then he filled the doll's bowl with pounded yams.

He set the little doll at the foot of a flamboyant tree where fairies like to dance. Ananse tied one end of a vine round the doll's head and, holding the other end in his hand, he hid behind a bush.

In a little while, Mmoatia the fairy-whom-no-man-sees came dancing, dancing, dancing, to the foot of the flamboyant tree. There she saw the doll holding the bowl of yams.

Mmoatia said: "Gum baby, I am hungry. May I eat some of your yams?"

Ananse pulled at the vine in his hiding place, so that the doll seemed to nod its head. So the fairy took the bowl from the doll and ate all the yams.

"Thank you, Gum baby," said the fairy. But the doll did not answer.

"Don't you reply when I thank you?" cried the angered fairy. The doll did not stir.

"Gum baby, I'll slap your crying place unless you answer me," shouted the fairy. But the wooden doll remained still and silent. So the fairy slapped her crying place—pa! Her hand stuck fast to the gum baby's sticky cheek.

"Let go of my hand, or I'll slap you again."—Pa! She slapped the doll's crying place with her other hand. Now the fairy was stuck to the gum baby with both hands, and she was furious. She pushed against the doll with her feet, and they also stuck fast.

Now Ananse came out of hiding. "You are ready to meet the Sky God, Mmoatia." And he carried her to the tree where the leopard and the hornets were waiting.

Ananse spun a web round Osebo, Mmboro, and Mmoatia. Then he spun a web to the sky. He pulled up his captives behind him, and set them down at the feet of the Sky God.

"O, Nyame," said Ananse, bowing low, "here is the price you ask for your stories: Osebo the leopard-of-the-terrible-teeth, Mmboro the hornets-who-sting-like-fire, and Mmoatia the fairy-whom-men-never-see."

Nyame the Sky God called together all the nobles of his court and addressed them in a loud voice: "Little Ananse, the spider man, has paid me the price I ask for my stories. Sing his praise. I command you."

"From this day and going on forever," proclaimed the Sky God, "my stories belong to Ananse and shall be called 'Spider Stories.' "

"Eeeee, Eeeee, Eeeee," shouted all the assembled nobles.

So Ananse took the golden box of stories back to earth, to the people of his village. And when he opened the box all the stories scattered to the corners of the world, including this one.

This is my story which I have related. If it be sweet, or if it be not sweet, take some elsewhere, and let some come back to me.

JOHNNY APPLESEED

retold and illustrated
by Steven Kellogg

John Chapman, who later became known as Johnny Appleseed, was born on September 26, 1774, when the apples on the trees surrounding his home in Leominster, Massachusetts, were as red as the autumn leaves.

John's first years were hard. His father left the family to fight in the Revolutionary War, and his mother and his baby brother both died before his second birthday.

By the time John turned six, his father had remarried and settled in Longmeadow, Massachusetts. Within a decade their little house was overflowing with ten more children.

Nearby was an apple orchard. Like most early American families, the Chapmans picked their apples in the fall,

stored them in the cellar for winter eating, and used them to make sauces, cider, vinegar, and apple butter. John loved to watch the spring blossoms slowly turn into the glowing fruit of autumn.

Watching the apples grow inspired in John a love of all of nature. He often escaped from his boisterous household to the tranquil woods. The animals sensed his gentleness and trusted him.

As soon as John was old enough to leave home, he set out to explore the vast wilderness to the west. When he reached the Allegheny Mountains, he cleared a plot of land and planted a small orchard with the pouch of apple seeds he had carried with him.

John walked hundreds of miles through the Pennsylvania forest, living like the Indians he befriended on the trail. As he traveled, he cleared the land for many more orchards. He was sure the pioneer families would be arriving before long, and he looked forward to supplying them with apple trees.

When a storm struck, he found shelter in a hollow log or built a lean-to. On clear nights he stretched out under the stars.

Over the next few years, John continued to visit and care for his new orchards. The winters slowed him down, but he survived happily on a diet of butternuts.

One spring he met a band of men who boasted that they could lick their weight in wildcats. They were amazed to hear that John wouldn't hurt an animal and had no use for a gun.

They challenged John to compete at wrestling, the favorite frontier sport. He suggested a more practical contest—a tree-chopping match. The woodsmen eagerly agreed.

When the sawdust settled, there was no question about who had come out on top.

John was pleased that the land for his largest orchard had been so quickly cleared. He thanked the exhausted woodsmen for their help and began planting.

During the next few years, John continued to move westward. Whenever he ran out of apple seeds, he hiked to the eastern cider presses to replenish his supply. Before long, John's plantings were spread across the state of Ohio.

Meanwhile, pioneer families were arriving in search of homesites and farmland. John had located his orchards on the routes he thought they'd be traveling. As he had hoped, the settlers were eager to buy his young trees.

John went out of his way to lend a helping hand to his new neighbors. Often he would give his trees away. People affectionately called him Johnny Appleseed, and he began using that name.

He particularly enjoyed entertaining children with tales of his wilderness adventures and stories from the Bible.

In 1812 the British incited the Indians to join them in another war against the Americans. The settlers feared that Ohio would be invaded from Lake Erie.

It grieved Johnny that his friends were fighting each other. But when he saw the smoke of burning cabins, he ran through the night, shouting a warning at every door.

After the war, people urged Johnny to build a house and settle down. He replied that he lived like a king in his wilderness home, and he returned to the forest he loved.

During his long absences, folks enjoyed sharing their recollections of Johnny. They retold his stories and sometimes they even exaggerated them a bit.

Some recalled Johnny sleeping in a treetop hammock and chatting with the birds.

Others remembered that a rattle-snake had attacked his foot. Fortunately, Johnny's feet were as tough as elephant's hide, so the fangs didn't penetrate.

It was said that Johnny had once tended a wounded wolf and then kept him for a pet.

An old hunter swore he'd seen Johnny frolicking with a bear family.

The storytellers outdid each other with tall tales about his feats of survival in the untamed wilderness.

As the years passed, Ohio became too crowded for Johnny. He moved to the wilds of Indiana, where he continued to clear land for his orchards.

When the settlers began arriving, Johnny recognized some of the children who had listened to his stories. Now they had children of their own.

It made Johnny's old heart glad when they welcomed him as a beloved friend and asked to hear his tales again.

When Johnny passed seventy, it became difficult for him to keep up with his work. Then, in March of 1845, while trudging through a snowstorm near Fort Wayne, Indiana, he became ill for the first time in his life.

Johnny asked for shelter in a settler's cabin, and a few days later he died there.

Curiously, Johnny's stories continued to move westward without him. Folks maintained that they'd seen him in Illinois or that he'd greeted them in Missouri, Arkansas, or Texas. Others were certain that he'd planted trees on the slopes of the Rocky Mountains or in California's distant valleys.

Even today people still claim they've seen Johnny Appleseed.

MEET STEVEN KELLOGG, AUTHOR AND ILLUSTRATOR

"The legends that grew around John Chapman began during his lifetime, and succeeding generations continued to enlarge and embellish them until the well-known and well-loved Johnny Appleseed was created. I tried to weave incidents and images to incorporate the recorded events in the life of John Chapman, the hardy, eccentric, and enterprising frontier fruit grower, with the tales that have evolved about Johnny Appleseed, the heroic and most gentle and generous of America's mythic figures."

A TALE OF THE BROTHERS GRIMM

Terry Fertig

illustrated by Bonnie MacKain

The Brothers Grimm. You've heard of them. Certainly you've heard their stories—"Cinderella," "Little Red-Riding-Hood," "Rumpelstiltskin." But who were they? And why are they so famous?

Jacob and Wilhelm Grimm were born in the German town of Hanau more than two hundred years ago—Jacob on January 4, 1785, and Wilhelm just over one year later on February 24, 1786. The Grimm family was a closely knit one—loving and loyal. Jacob and Wilhelm were the oldest of six children. Because they were so close in age, the two brothers were close in heart as well—very much like twins. They did everything together. They played together; they ate together; they took long walks together. They read the same books and often studied at the same desk.

But when Jacob was eleven and Wilhelm was ten, their father died. Being the oldest, the two boys helped hold the family together during this difficult time for their mother. Two years later, however, the two brothers left their family and moved to the town of Cassel in order to continue their schooling. It seemed the days of their childhood were over.

Although they missed their mother, the boys did well in school and soon went on to the university in Marburg, where they decided to study law. As we all know, however, the Brothers Grimm did not become famous lawyers. Instead they followed a different path to fame—one that involved books, stories, language, and tradition. They became collectors of folklore, preservers of old tales.

There were two main reasons why the brothers chose the path they did. First, while at the university, Jacob and Wilhelm became friends with a professor who owned a collection of ancient books from medieval times. They enjoyed spending time at his home studying these wonderful old books and manuscripts. In this way, the brothers became fascinated with old German literature and

the stories, songs, and ballads of the common people that they discovered in these old books.

The second reason why the brothers chose the work they did had to do with the times in which they lived. What was happening in Europe at the time affected them greatly and sparked them to collect the fairy tales for which they are now so well known.

You see, during nearly twenty years of the brothers' childhood and young adult life, a great many changes were taking place in Europe. It was a very troubled time. There were political struggles and wars being fought. The people of France had revolted against their government, and war continued there for many years. Napoleon, a French general, eventually seized power in France, crowned himself emperor, and set out to conquer most of Europe. After a time, Napoleon was successful in conquering many lands—including Germany.

Such activity was very disturbing for all Europeans, and the Grimm brothers were no exception. They were patriotic young men who had become most interested in their German heritage—the customs and traditions of their country and its people. With the French army attacking and conquering what seemed to be all of Europe, Jacob and Wilhelm feared that much of their German culture would be lost and forgotten.

And so their interest in the oral tradition—the stories that had been told and passed down through the generations—and their fear that these stories might be lost caused the brothers to begin researching and collecting fairy tales.

Since the brothers did not have the tape recorders and other electronic equipment that we have today, they wrote by hand every word of every story they were told. Recording these stories, therefore, was not easy. So much of good storytelling depends on the storyteller's voice—raising and lowering it at a meaningful moment, putting a pause at just the right spot, or adding a bit of an accent or dialect. These are the kinds of things that make stories special but are hard to write down.

Wilhelm was an expert with language, however, and was able to improve the stories by writing simpler sentences, using repeated words, adding vivid descriptions, and inserting dialogue. Of course Wilhelm worked under the watchful eye of brother Jacob, who insisted that the tales remain true to their original form. But Wilhelm's poetic way with words simply made the tales more childlike, more enchanting, more magical. And children loved them.

The brothers also discovered that it was difficult to find storytellers willing to tell their tales. First, there weren't many who still knew the old tales and could tell them well. Back in the Middle Ages, many people made a living telling stories. They entertained at weddings and other festivals. But when type was invented and stories were printed for people to read, these professional storytellers began to disappear. Storytelling then became an activity that continued mainly in country areas. And second, of the storytellers the brothers found, few would agree to tell their stories. Usually such stories were told at family get-togethers or to children. The storytellers could not believe that two educated gentlemen would want to hear such tales. They were certain they'd be laughed at.

But Jacob and Wilhelm were determined to collect as many old tales as they could. They used their wits and often bartered for stories when they thought it would work. One old soldier in particular was thrilled to trade a tale or two for an old pair of pants.

Members of the Wild family were especially helpful. They had been the Grimms' next-door neighbors in Cassel. Dorothea Wild, who would later become Wilhelm's wife, was an excellent storyteller, as were Gretchen, Lisette, and

Mamma. But from that household, the Wilds' old nanny, Marie, was by far the best. It was Marie who told the brothers the tales of "Snow White," "Little Red-Riding-Hood," and "The Sleeping Beauty."

Begun in 1806, the first volume of fairy tales, titled *Nursery and Household Tales*, was published in 1812. The brothers had written the tales mainly for adults to read *to* their children—slowly, one at a time, so that they could enjoy every word. But children loved to read them as well and, for some, the book could not be torn from their hands.

The fairy tales of Jacob and Wilhelm Grimm helped bring national pride back to the people of Germany. But maybe these stories were enjoyed more because they allowed readers to escape from the troubled times in which they lived. In any case, the Grimm brothers decided, to the delight of their readers, to continue collecting stories for a second volume and eventually a third.

The second time around, the brothers had less trouble finding willing storytellers. In fact the first book of *Household Tales* became so famous that people now came to them with stories. One day they were lucky enough to meet what they called a "genuine storyteller." Her name was Frau Katharina Dorothea Viehmann, but they nicknamed her the Fairytale-Wife. She was a widow who sold eggs and butter in the small village where she lived with her children and grandchildren. Often she told stories to villagers in exchange for a bowl of soup or a cup of coffee.

She had a real gift for telling tales and would repeat them, exactly the same each time, so that they could be written down word for word. Friends knew what a great find she would be for Jacob and Wilhelm and so persuaded her to visit them. The brothers welcomed her warmly with hot coffee and sweets, and she shared with them more than twenty old tales. How fortunate that Jacob and Wilhelm were able to save her precious stories when they did. Frau Viehmann died less than one year after the second book of fairy tales was published.

The most famous of Frau Viehmann's stories was "Cinderella," which came from an old French tale called

"The Little Fur Slipper." Since the French word for fur, *vair*, and the French word for glass, *verre*, are pronounced the same, the fur slipper became a glass slipper in the Grimms' book of fairy tales. Because these tales had always been told and retold rather than read from a book, it's easy to see how such a change could happen.

Jacob and Wilhelm continued to work together side by side throughout their lifetime. Even after Wilhelm married Dorothea Wild, Jacob remained in their house and was a loving uncle to their three children. Jacob and Wilhelm still took long walks together and cooperated on many writing projects, often signing their books as one—Brothers Grimm. Besides the fairy tales they collected, the brothers published a book of German folk tales. Folk tales are different from fairy tales. Fairy tales are usually about fantasy and magic. Folk tales are more realistic, often based on a real place or event in history. By preserving these jewels of German heritage, the Grimm brothers brought honor to their country.

Wilhelm Grimm died in 1859. Jacob died four years later. They are buried next to each other in Berlin. They became folk heroes in their country—very much like the characters in the tales they collected. *Grimms' Fairy Tales* has been translated into nearly seventy languages. Without the Brothers Grimm, the magical world of fairy tales might have been lost forever.

WORLDS I KNOW

Myra Cohn Livingston
illustrated by Heidi Chang

I can read the pictures
by myself
in the books that lie
on the lowest shelf.
I know the place
where the stories start
and some I can even say
by heart,
and I make up adventures
and dreams and words
for some of the pages
I've never heard.

But I like it best
when Mother sits
and reads to me
my favorites;
when Rapunzel pines
and the prince comes forth,
or the Snow Queen sighs
in the bitter north;
when Rose Red snuggles
against the bear,
and I lean against Mother
and feel her hair.

We look at stars
in Hungary—
back of the North Wind—
over the sea—
the Nutcracker laughs;
the Erl King calls;
a wish comes true;
the beanstalk falls;
the Western wind
blows sweet and low,
and Mother gives words
to worlds I know.

All photographs ©Lawrence Migdale

CARVING THE POLE

from TOTEM POLE
by Diane Hoyt-Goldsmith
photographs by Lawrence Migdale

My name is David. I live in a small town called Kingston in Washington State. In the summer, I like to hunt for salmonberries and blackberries in the fields near our house.

My father is an artist, a wood-carver. Ever since I was little, I have watched him take a piece of wood and carve a creature from it. Sometimes it is a wolf, sometimes a bear, and sometimes an eagle. The eagle is the symbol and totem of the Eagle Clan, which is our family group within our tribe.

My father is carving a totem pole for the Klallam Indians who live on the Port Gamble Reservation near our home. Although my father belongs to a different tribe, the Tsimshian, he was asked to carve the pole because of his skill. It is common among the Northwest Coast Indians for one tribe to invite an artist from another tribe to carve a pole for them. The pole will be made from a single log, forty feet long. It will have animals and figures carved on it, important characters from Klallam myths and legends.

My father says that a totem pole is like a signboard. He tells me that it is a system for passing on legends and stories from one generation to another for people who have no written language. A totem pole is like a library for a tribe!

David and his father look for a tall, straight tree in the woods near their home.

The first step in making a totem pole is to find a straight tree. It must be wide enough to make a strong pole. The best trees for a totem pole have few branches. Where a branch joins the trunk a knot forms, making the carving very difficult.

Nearly all totem poles are carved from cedar logs. Cedar trees grow very straight and are common in the evergreen forests along the coastline near our home. The wood of the cedar is soft and easy to carve. It does not rot and insects will not destroy it. A totem pole carved from a cedar log can last a hundred years or more.

After the right tree is found and cut down, all the branches are removed with an axe and the bark is stripped from the outside of the log. In the old days, the Indians had no saws or axes, so even cutting the tree down was a harder job than it is today. Back then, the carvers used a hammer and chisel to cut a wedge at the base of the tree. This weakened the tree, and in a strong wind storm, the tree would fall.

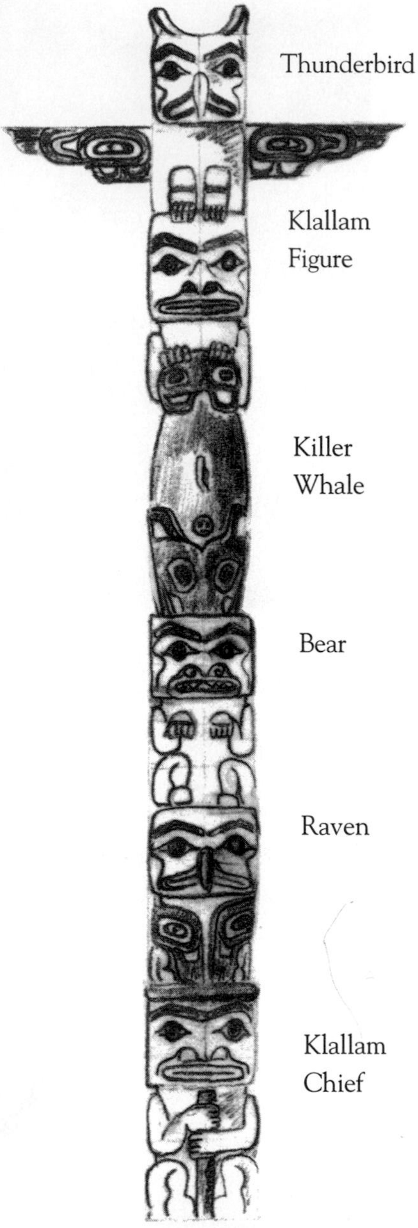

When the log is ready to be carved, my father makes a drawing of how the pole will look when it is finished. He draws the animals for the totem pole on a sheet of paper. He might begin by drawing each animal separately, but before he starts to carve he will draw a picture of how the completed pole will look.

Next he uses a stick of charcoal to make a drawing on the log itself. Then he stands up on the log to see how the figures and animals look. When he is satisfied with the drawing, he takes up his tools and begins to carve.

The totem pole for the Klallam tribe has six figures, one on top of the other. At the very top of the pole is the Thunderbird. He brings good luck to the Klallam village. The Klallam people believe the Thunderbird lives on the Olympic mountain range, across the water from their reservation, in the place where the mountains touch the sky. They say that when Thunderbird catches the great Killer Whale, you can hear thunder and see lightning in the sky.

Below Thunderbird is the figure who represents the Klallam people. The figure holds Killer Whale by the tail. Together, they tell the legend of a tribal member named Charlie who rode out to sea on the back of a Killer Whale.

The fourth animal on the pole is Bear, who provided the Indian people with many important things. His fur gave warmth and clothing. His meat gave food. His claws and teeth were used for trinkets and charms and to decorate clothing.

The next figure is Raven, who brought light to the Indian people by stealing the Sun from Darkness. Raven is the great trickster. Sometimes he does things that are good, but sometimes he does things that are bad.

The last figure on the pole is a Klallam Chief. The chief on the pole holds a "speaker stick," a symbol of his leadership and his important position in the tribe. In the Klallam culture, when a chief holds the speaker stick, all the people pay attention and listen to what he says.

As my father carves the pole, he brings all of these characters to life. He works on the pole every day. He uses many tools: the adze, chisels, and handmade knives. He even uses a chain saw for the largest cuts!

This totem pole is special to me. I am finally old enough to help my father with the work. He lets me sweep away the wood shavings as he carves. I can also take care of the tools he uses—the adze, the saws, the handmade knives, and the chisels.

As I get older, I'll learn how to use my father's carving tools safely and to help him really carve a pole. But for now, I just practice on some bits of wood I find lying around. Like my father, I look for the animal shapes hidden inside the wood.

David's father carves a totem pole on the Klallam Reservation. He works from a drawing which he transfers onto the log. The charcoal outline of the Bear's eyebrows are visible on the wood.

David and his father walk along the pole to check the progress of the carving. Kneeling on top, David learns to judge whether the figures on the pole are lined up correctly.

Striking the wood with the adze makes a unique pattern on the pole. This pattern differs with every carver and is like a signature of the artist who carves the pole.

Using a handmade knife, David's father carves fine details into the pole.

David paints the eye shape of the Klallam Figure black.

This box was made by David's great-great-grandfather as a storage box for food. Now David's father uses it as a toolbox. The adzes in front are made from the elbows of alder or yew tree branches.

In the old days, it used to take a year to carve a totem pole. In those days, the blade of the adze was made of stone and wasn't nearly as sharp as the steel blades my father uses today. Knives, for the carving of fine details, were made from beaver teeth or from large shells.

My father says that it is the artist's skill with the adze that makes a totem pole great. Each artist has his own way of carving. The strokes of the adze create a pattern in the wood, like small ripples across the wide water.

In the old days, carvers had special songs to chant while they worked. The chanting helped them keep up a rhythm with their adzing strokes. Now my father likes to work to songs on the radio. He works to the beat of rock 'n' roll.

My father makes the work look easy. He cuts into the wood quickly, as if it were as soft as soap. I know carving is much harder than he makes it look. I know because I've tried it.

After all the figures and animals are carved into the log, I help my father paint the pole. We make the eyes dark. We paint the mouths red. Whale's back and dorsal fin are black. Raven and Thunderbird have wings with patterns of red and black. The colors my father shows me are taken from the old traditions of the Tsimshian people. From a distance, the pole will look powerful and strong.

Finally, after two months of hard work, my father puts away his tools and packs up his paintbrushes. The totem pole is finished.

The completed totem pole greets travelers who journey to the Klallam Reservation. The figures on the pole are Thunderbird at the top, then a Klallam Figure holding Killer Whale by the tail, then Bear, Raven, and the Klallam Chief with his speaker stick.

ORAL HISTORY

T. Marie Kryst

illustrated by David Cunningham

The first people to keep records and write down the history and stories of their ancestors were probably the ancient Egyptians and the Chinese. But what about before that, before people even knew how to write? How did people keep family information?

Members of a clan or tribe gathered around campfires and recited poetry and sang songs. Many of these songs and poems told about family history. Important names, brave deeds, and memorable events were passed on to younger members of the group, who remembered and memorized them for safekeeping. This is called oral history because it is history that is passed on by word of mouth instead of being written down. It was the only way of keeping family records before there was writing.

However, oral history thrives even today. The stories we hear from parents and grandparents as they remember the past are good examples of oral history in action. In certain areas of the world—Africa and some Pacific islands, for instance—oral history survives in a much more formal way. Many tribes or groups in West Africa have a griot, or village member who can recite the history of all the families in the village. If he should die, another has been trained to take his place so that history is not lost.

One report tells of a New Zealand tribal chief who had to recite the story of his people—thirty-four generations worth—in order to prove his right to land he had inherited. Some say his retelling took three days!

Another account tells of the longest oral history ever recited, covering seventy generations. This retelling was by an old man on an Indonesian island.

Island people are the most likely to have spoken records that go back such a long way. On an island, families are not as likely to move very far away, making it easier to keep track of family history.

However, if history, including family stories, is not remembered and retold, it will die out. In 1966, a group of high school students in Rabun Gap, Georgia, began a project that has become a well-known and much copied example of recording oral history. These students collected stories, songs, and mountain folklore from neighbors, family members, and other people who lived in their part of the

Appalachian Mountains. They recorded traditional crafts and skills, such as banjo making and bear hunting. These spoken memories were published as a magazine called *Foxfire*. As the project continued every year, the magazine grew and became a series of Foxfire books. With these books, the students saved the rich history of an important piece of American life that might otherwise have been lost.

You can save your family's history, too. It's important to record what older members of the family remember so that your family's story won't be lost and forgotten. Here's how to begin:

1. First, make a list of three or four of the oldest living members of your family—great-grandparents or great-aunts and uncles would be wonderful. These might be people you've never met or don't know very well. Your parents can probably help.
2. Next, make a phone call or write a short note asking if they would be willing to talk with you about what they remember about their ancestors. If they live far away, you might ask them to write down any memories or information they think would be useful and send it to you by mail.
3. Find out from them if they know any other family members who might be helpful to you.
4. Make a list of questions that you want to have answered. This is a good way to spark their memories. But also let

them just talk and tell stories about the past. They will enjoy it, and you will get some interesting information.

5. Record what these family members say. A tape recorder is usually the best way to do this, but you can also take notes. Get as many details as you can, such as first and middle names, parents' names, place names, and exact dates. This will help if you search for written records later.

You will still have a lot of work to do if you decide to continue your search. But this use of oral history will get you started on the road to piecing together the story of your family.

AUNT FLOSSIE'S HATS

(AND CRAB CAKES LATER)

Elizabeth Fitzgerald Howard
illustrated by James Ransome

On Sunday afternoons, Sarah and I go to see Great-great-aunt Flossie. Sarah and I love Aunt Flossie's house. It is crowded full of stuff and things. Books and pictures and lamps and pillows . . . Plates and trays and old dried flowers . . . And boxes and boxes and boxes of HATS!

On Sunday afternoon when Sarah and I go to see Aunt Flossie, she says, "Come in, Susan. Come in, Sarah. Have some tea. Have some cookies. Later we can get some crab cakes!"

We sip our tea and eat our cookies, and then Aunt Flossie lets us look in her hatboxes.

We pick out hats and try them on. Aunt Flossie says they are her memories, and each hat has its story.

Hats, hats, hats, hats! A stiff black one with bright red ribbons. A soft brown one with silver buttons. Thin floppy hats that hide our eyes. Green or blue or pink or purple. Some have fur and some have feathers. Look! This hat is

just one smooth soft rose, but here's one with a trillion flowers! Aunt Flossie has so many hats!

One Sunday afternoon, I picked out a wooly winter hat, sort of green, maybe. Aunt Flossie thought a minute. Aunt Flossie almost always thinks a minute before she starts a hat story. Then she sniffed the wooly hat. "Just a little smoky smell now," she said.

Sarah and I sniffed the hat, too. "Smoky smell, Aunt Flossie?"

"The big fire," Aunt Flossie said. "The big fire in Baltimore. Everything smelled of smoke for miles around. For days and days. Big fire. Didn't come near our house on Centre Street, but we could hear fire engines racing down St. Paul. Horses' hooves clattering. Bells! Whistles! Your great-grandma and I couldn't sleep. We grabbed our coats

and hats and ran outside. Worried about Uncle Jimmy's grocery store, worried about the terrapins and crabs. Big fire in Baltimore."

Aunt Flossie closed her eyes. I think she was seeing long ago. I wondered about crab cakes. Did they have crab cakes way back then? Then Sarah sniffed Aunt Flossie's hat. "No more smoky smell," she said. But I thought I could smell some, just a little.

Then Sarah tried a different hat. Dark, dark blue, with a red feather. "This one, Aunt Flossie! This one!"

Aunt Flossie closed her eyes and thought a minute. "Oh my, yes, my, my. What an exciting day!"

We waited, Sarah and I. "What happened, Aunt Flossie?" I asked.

"Big parade in Baltimore."

"Ooh! Parade!" said Sarah. "We love parades."

"I made that hat," Aunt Flossie said, "to wear to watch that big parade. Buglers bugling. Drummers drumming. Flags flying everywhere. The boys—soldiers, you know—back from France. Marching up Charles Street. Proud. Everyone cheering, everyone shouting! The Great War was over! The Great War was over!"

"Let's have a parade!" I said. Sarah put on the dark blue hat. I found a red one with a furry pompom. We marched around Aunt Flossie's house.

"March with us, Aunt Flossie!" I called. But she was closing her eyes. She was seeing long ago. "Maybe she's dreaming about crab cakes," Sarah said.

Then we looked in the very special box. "Look, Aunt Flossie! Here's your special hat." It was the big straw hat with the pink and yellow flowers and green velvet ribbon. Aunt Flossie's favorite best Sunday hat! It's our favorite story, because we are in the story, and we can help Aunt Flossie tell it!

Aunt Flossie smiled. "One Sunday afternoon," she said, "we were going out for crab cakes. Sarah and Susan . . ."

"And Mommy and Daddy," I said.

"And Aunt Flossie," said Sarah.

Aunt Flossie nodded. "We were walking by the water. And the wind came."

"Let me tell it," I said. "The wind came and blew away your favorite best Sunday hat!"

"My favorite best Sunday hat," said Aunt Flossie. "It landed in the water."

"It was funny," said Sarah.

"I didn't think so," said Aunt Flossie.

"And Daddy tried to reach it," I said, "but he slid down in the mud. Daddy looked really surprised, and everybody laughed."

"He couldn't rescue my favorite, favorite best Sunday hat," said Aunt Flossie.

"And Mommy got a stick and leaned far out. She almost fell in, but she couldn't reach it either. The water rippled, and your favorite best Sunday hat just floated by like a boat!"

"Now comes the best part, and I'll tell it!" said Sarah. "A big brown dog came. It was walking with a boy. 'May we help you?' the boy asked. 'My dog Gretchen can get it.' The boy threw a small, small stone. It landed in Aunt Flossie's hat! 'Fetch, Gretchen, fetch! Fetch, Gretchen, fetch!' Gretchen jumped into the water and she swam. She swam and she got it! Gretchen got Aunt Flossie's hat! 'Hurray for Gretchen!' We all jumped up and down. 'Hurray for Aunt Flossie's hat!' "

"It was very wet," said Aunt Flossie. "but it dried just fine . . . almost like new. My favorite, favorite best Sunday hat."

"I like that story," I said.

"So do I," said Sarah. "And I like what happened next! We went to get crab cakes!"

"Crab cakes!" said Aunt Flossie. "What a wonderful idea! Sarah, Susan, telephone your parents. We'll go get some crab cakes right now!"

I think Sarah and I will always agree about one thing: Nothing in the whole wide world tastes as good as crab cakes.

But crab cakes taste best after stories . . . stories about Aunt Flossie's hats!

MEET ELIZABETH FITZGERALD HOWARD, AUTHOR

The idea for Aunt Flossie's Hats *came from one of Elizabeth Fitzgerald Howard's fond memories—a family visit to the Inner Harbour in Baltimore. There the real Aunt Flossie lost her "favorite best Sunday hat" to the wind, resulting in a mad scramble to retrieve it. Howard's Aunt Flossie Wright was a Baltimore school teacher who "lived in the same house most of her life," "knew everyone," and "never threw anything away." Howard says her Aunt Flossie always had stories to tell about the old days.*

MEET JAMES RANSOME, ILLUSTRATOR

James Ransome enjoys illustrating books for children. "I try to add things to the illustration that the writer couldn't put in the story. Aunt Flossie liked to collect things so I tried to put a lot of old things in the house—paintings of old relatives, china, and other knick-knacks." Color is also important to Ransome. "I used earth tones to give the feeling that Aunt Flossie is a down-to-earth person with a lot of respect for family, someone you'd admire."

THE KEEPING QUILT

Patricia Polacco

When my Great-Gramma Anna came to America, she wore the same thick overcoat and big boots she had worn for farm work. But her family weren't dirt farmers anymore. In New York City her father's work was hauling things on a wagon, and the rest of the family made artificial flowers all day.

Everyone was in a hurry, and it was so crowded, not like in backhome Russia. But all the same it was their home, and most of their neighbors were just like them.

When Anna went to school, English sounded to her like pebbles dropping into shallow water. *Shhhhhh. . . . Shhhhhh. . . . Shhhhhh.* In six months she was speaking English. Her parents almost never learned, so she spoke English for them, too.

The only things she had left of backhome Russia were her dress and the babushka she liked to throw up into the air when she was dancing.

And her dress was getting too small. After her mother had sewn her a new one, she took her old dress and babushka. Then from a basket of old clothes she took Uncle Vladimir's shirt, Aunt Havalah's nightdress, and an apron of Aunt Natasha's.

"We will make a quilt to help us always remember home," Anna's mother said. "It will be like having the family in backhome Russia dance around us at night."

And so it was. Anna's mother invited all the neighborhood ladies. They cut out animals and flowers from the scraps of clothing. Anna kept the needles threaded and handed them to the ladies as they needed them. The border of the quilt was made of Anna's babushka.

On Friday nights Anna's mother would say the prayers that started the Sabbath. The family ate challah and chicken soup. The quilt was the tablecloth.

Anna grew up and fell in love with Great-Grandpa Sasha. To show he wanted to be her husband, he gave Anna a gold coin, a dried flower, and a piece of rock salt, all tied into a linen handkerchief. The gold was for wealth, the flower for love, and the salt so their lives would have flavor.

She accepted the hankie. They were engaged.

Under the wedding huppa, Anna and Sasha promised each other love and understanding. After the wedding, the men and women celebrated separately.

When my Grandma Carle was born, Anna wrapped her daughter in the quilt to welcome her warmly into the world. Carle was given a gift of gold, flower, salt, and bread.

Gold so she would never know poverty, a flower so she would always know love, salt so her life would always have flavor, and bread so that she would never know hunger.

Carle learned to keep the Sabbath and to cook and clean and do washing.

"Married you'll be someday," Anna told Carle, and . . . again the quilt became a wedding huppa, this time for Carle's wedding to Grandpa George. Men and women celebrated together, but they still did not dance together. In Carle's wedding bouquet was a gold coin, bread, and salt.

Carle and George moved to a farm in Michigan and Great-Gramma Anna came to live with them. The quilt once again wrapped a new little girl, Mary Ellen.

Mary Ellen called Anna, Lady Gramma. She had grown very old and was sick a lot of the time. The quilt kept her legs warm.

On Anna's ninety-eighth birthday, the cake was a kulich, a rich cake with raisins and candied fruit in it.

When Great-Gramma Anna died, prayers were said to lift her soul to heaven. My mother Mary Ellen was now grown up.

When Mary Ellen left home, she took the quilt with her.

When she became a bride, the quilt became her huppa. For the first time, friends who were not Jews came to the wedding. My mother wore a suit, but in her bouquet were gold, bread, and salt.

The quilt welcomed me, Patricia, into the world . . . and it was the tablecloth for my first birthday party.

At night I would trace my fingers around the edges of each animal on the quilt before I went to sleep. I told my mother stories about the animals on the quilt. She told me

whose sleeve had made the horse, whose apron had made the chicken, whose dress had made the flowers, and whose babushka went around the edge of the quilt.

The quilt was a pretend cape when I was in the bullring, or sometimes a tent in the steaming Amazon jungle.

At my wedding to Enzo-Mario, men and women danced together. In my bouquet were gold, bread, and salt—and a sprinkle of wine, so I would always know laughter.

Twenty years ago I held Traci Denise in the quilt for the first time. Someday she, too, will leave home and she will take the quilt with her.

MEET PATRICIA POLACCO, AUTHOR AND ILLUSTRATOR

Patricia Polacco has fond feelings about her family, whom she describes as marvelous storytellers. She says, "My fondest memories are of sitting around a stove or open fire, eating apples and popping corn while listening to the old ones tell glorious stories about the past. . . . With each retelling our stories gained a little more UMPH!"

The Keeping Quilt *is a true story about Polacco's great-grandmother Anna and the quilt Anna's mother made from the family's old clothes so that Anna would always remember the old country.*

FINE ART
STORYTELLING

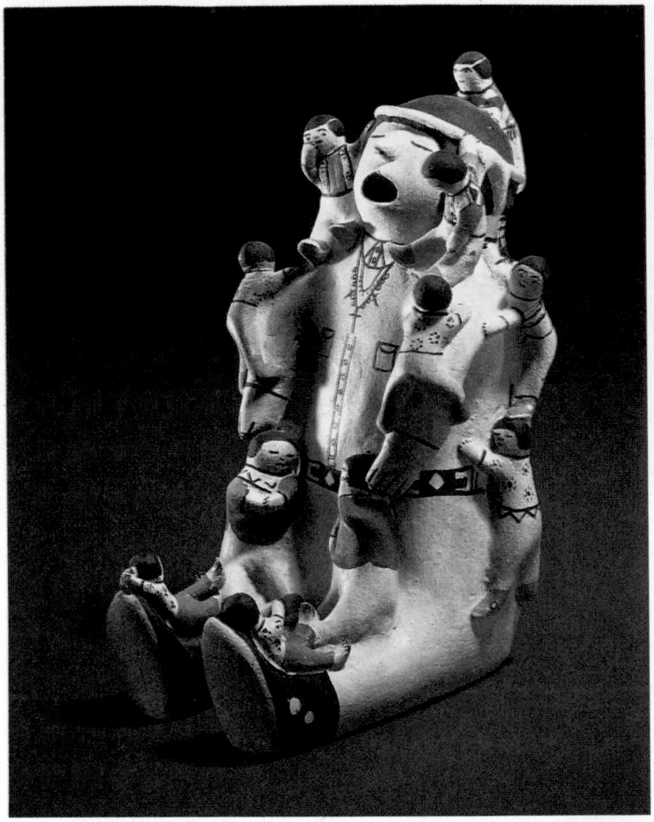

Pueblo Storyteller. 1969. Helen Cordero.

Cochiti Pueblo. Clay sculpture. 13" high. Heard Museum, Phoenix, Arizona. Photo: © Jerry Jacka

Bayeux Tapestry. 1070–1080. Artists unknown.

Embroidered wool on linen. Musée de Peinture, Bayeux, France

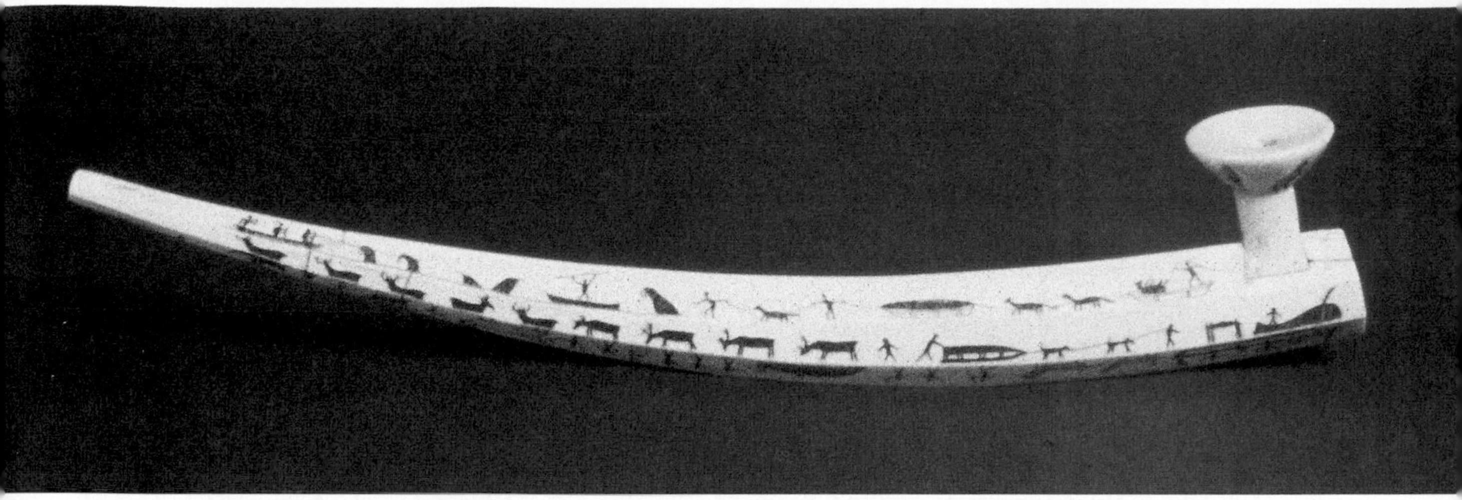

Carved walrus ivory pipe stem. c. 1850.
Eskimo, Kotzebue.

The National Museum of the American Indian, Smithsonian Institution. 3312

Member of Parliament and the Medjeles. 1834. Horace Vernet.

Oil on canvas. Musée Condé, Chantilly, France. Photo: Giraudon/Art Resource

AUNT SUE'S STORIES

Langston Hughes
illustrated by Gavin Curtis

Aunt Sue has a head full of stories.
Aunt Sue has a whole heart full of stories.
Summer nights on the front porch
Aunt Sue cuddles a brown-faced child to her bosom
And tells him stories.

Black slaves
Working in the hot sun,
And black slaves
Walking in the dewy night,
And black slaves
Singing sorrow songs on the banks of a mighty river
Mingle themselves softly
In the flow of old Aunt Sue's voice,
Mingle themselves softly
In the dark shadows that cross and recross
Aunt Sue's stories.

And the dark-faced child, listening,
Knows that Aunt Sue's stories are real stories.
He knows that Aunt Sue
Never got her stories out of any book at all,
But that they came
Right out of her own life.

And the dark-faced child is quiet
Of a summer night
Listening to Aunt Sue's stories.

MEET LANGSTON HUGHES, POET

"My grandmother was very proud. . . . She sat . . . in her rocker and read the Bible, or held me on her lap and told me long, beautiful stories. . . . Through my grandmother's stories always life moved, moved heroically toward an end. Nobody ever cried in my grandmother's stories. They worked, or schemed, or fought. But no crying. When my grandmother died, I didn't cry, either. Something about my grandmother's stories (without her ever having said so) taught me the uselessness of crying about anything."

MEMORY

Mary O'Neill

Memory is a tape recorder
And there's one in every head
Storing everything we've ever seen,
Or felt, or heard, or said.
The word, *remember,* simply means
We're playing back a part
Of all that's been recorded there
And lives close to our heart.
Sad thing, sweet thing,
Whatever it be,
The calling it back is a
Memory.

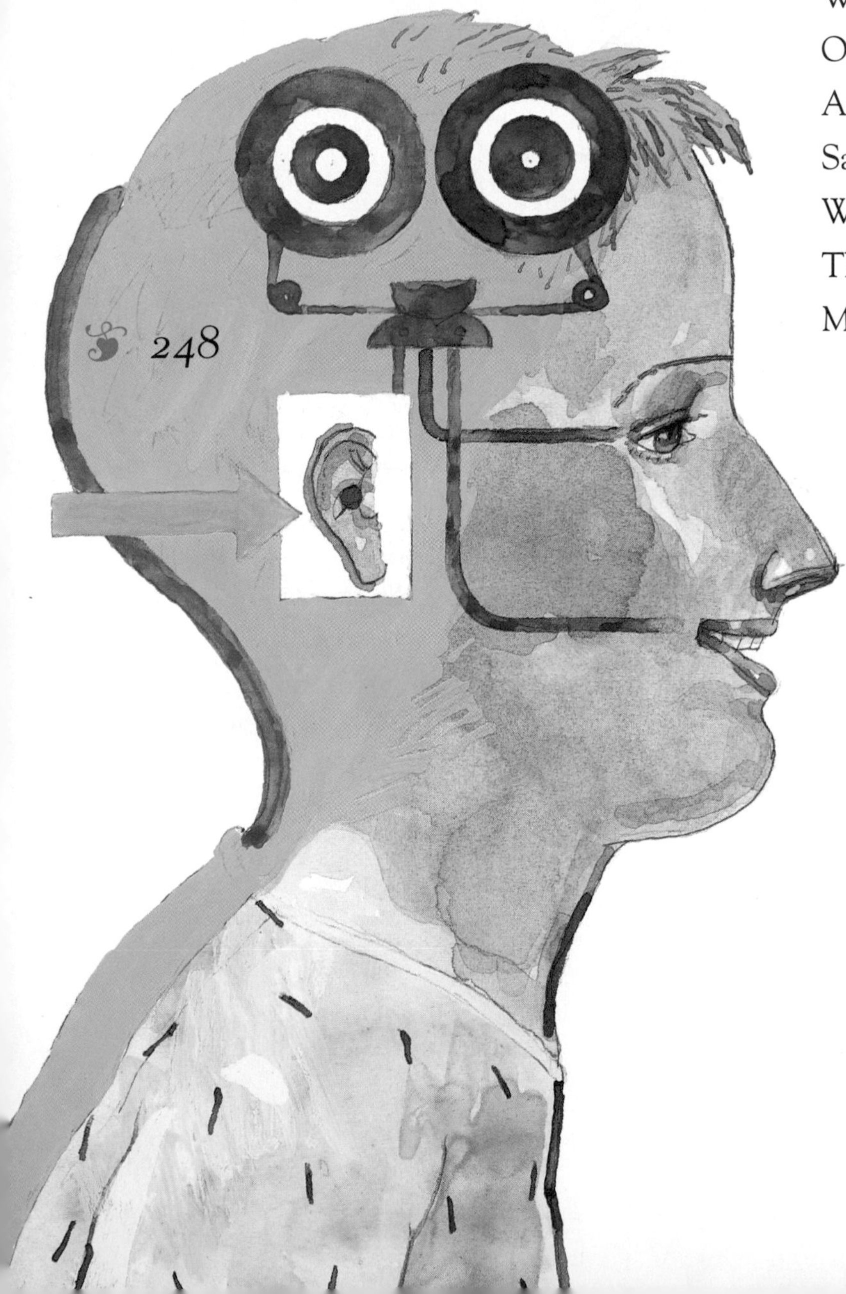

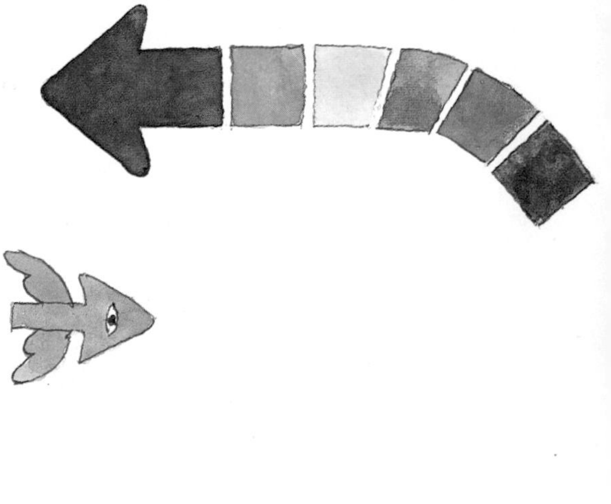

PAST
Arnold Adoff

I have all these parts   stuffed in
me
like mama's chicken
and
biscuits,
and
daddy's apple pie, and a tasty
story
from the family
tree.
But I know that tomorrow
morning
I'll wake up
empty, and hungry for that
next
bite
of my new
day.

illustrated by Friso Henstra

THE WALL

Eve Bunting

illustrated by Ronald Himler

This is the wall, my grandfather's wall. On it are the names of those killed in a war, long ago.

"Where is Grandpa's name?" I ask.

"We have to find it," Dad says.

He and I have come a long way for this and we walk slowly, searching.

The wall is black and shiny as a mirror. In it I can see Dad and me.

I can see the bare trees behind us and the dark, flying clouds.

A man in a wheelchair stares at the names. He doesn't have legs.

I'm looking, and he sees me looking and smiles.

"Hi, son."

"Hi."

His hat is a soft, squashed green and there are medals on it. His pant legs are folded back and his shirt is a soldier's shirt.

A woman old as my grandma is hugging a man, old as my grandpa would be. They are both crying.

"Sh," he whispers. "Sh!"

Flowers and other things have been laid against the wall.

There are little flags, an old teddy bear, and letters, weighted with stones so they won't blow away. Someone has left a rose with a droopy head.

“Have you found Grandpa yet?” I ask.

“No,” Dad says. “There are so many names. They are listed under the years when they were killed. I’ve found 1967.”

That’s when my grandpa died.

Dad runs his fingers along the rows of print and I do, too. The letters march side by side, like rows of soldiers. They’re nice and even. It’s better printing than I can do. The wall is warm.

Dad is searching and searching.

“Albert A. Jensen,

Charles Bronoski,

George Munoz,” he mutters.

His fingers stop moving. “Here he is.”

“My grandpa?” I ask.

Dad nods. “Your grandpa.” His voice blurs. “My dad. He was just my age when he was killed.”

Dad’s rubbing the name, rubbing and rubbing as if he wants to wipe it away. Maybe he just wants to remember the way it feels.

He lifts me so I can touch it, too.

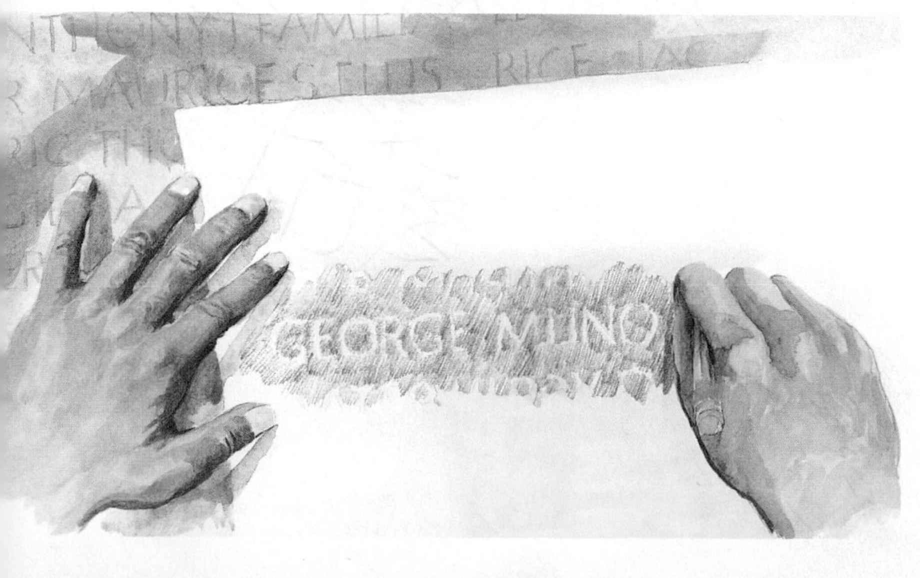

We’ve brought paper. Dad puts it over the letters and rubs on it with a pencil so the paper goes dark, and the letters show up white.

"You've got parts of other guys' names on there, too," I tell him.

Dad looks at the paper. "Your grandpa won't mind."

"They were probably friends of his anyway," I say.

Dad nods. "Maybe so."

A man and a boy walk past.

"Can we go to the river now, Grandpa?" the boy asks.

"Yes." The man takes the boy's hand. "But button your jacket. It's cold."

My dad stands very still with his head bent.

A bunch of big girls in school uniforms come down the path. Their teacher is with them. They are all carrying more of those little flags.

"Is this wall for the dead soldiers, Miss Gerber?" one of them asks in a loud voice.

"The names are the names of the dead. But the wall is for all of us," the teacher says.

They make a lot of noise and ask a lot of questions and all the time Dad just stands there with his head bowed, and I stand beside him.

The girls stick their flags in the dirt in front of the wall and leave.

Then it's quiet again.

Dad folds the paper that has Grandpa's name on it and puts it in his wallet. He slides out a picture of me, one of the yucky ones they took in school. Mom made me wear a tie.

Dad puts the picture on the grass below Grandpa's name.

It blows away.

I get it and put it back and pile some little stones on top. My face smiles up at me from under the stones.

"Grandpa won't know who I am," I tell Dad.

"I think he will," Dad says.

I move closer to him. "It's sad here."

He puts his hand on my shoulder. "I know. But it's a place of honor. I'm proud that your grandfather's name is on this wall."

"I am, too."

I am.

But I'd rather have my grandpa here, taking me to the river, telling me to button my jacket because it's cold.

I'd rather have him here.

NOTE

The Vietnam Veterans Memorial honors the men and women of the armed forces of the United States who served in the Vietnam War. On it are listed the names of those who gave their lives.

The Memorial is located in Washington, D.C. On the wall are more than 58,000 names, and other names are constantly being added as the remains of those "missing in action" are found.

MEET EVE BUNTING, AUTHOR

"It wasn't easy [to write this story]. It took three years from that first realization . . . to the finished text. In that time I wrote other books. But always, drifting somewhere in my conscious thoughts, was The Wall.

"Last year my husband and I went to Washington, D.C. I was scheduled to speak at a conference there but I had a pilgrimage to complete. One early morning we went to the Vietnam Veterans Memorial. I had brought the folded and gathered sheets, the first unbound copy of The Wall *complete with Ronald Himler's evocative art. I leaned it against the base of the dark, reflecting surface—*The Wall at The Wall*—wept, as so many people do there, and left. I knew the copy would go into the museum where all artifacts left at the memorial are kept. I liked that.*

"What the book says is true. The names on The Wall *are the names of the dead. But* The Wall *is for all of us."*

HOME PLACE

Crescent Dragonwagon
illustrated by Jerry Pinkney

Every year,
these daffodils come up.
There is no house near them.
There is nobody to water them.
Unless somebody happens to come this way,
like us, this Sunday afternoon, just walking,
there is not even anyone to see them.
But still they come up, these daffodils
in a row, a yellow splash
brighter than sunlight, or lamplight, or butter,
in the green and shadow of the woods.
Still they come up, these daffodils,
cups lifted to trumpet
the good news
of spring,

though maybe no one hears
except the wind
and the raccoons who rustle at night
and the deer who nibble delicately
at the new green growth
and the squirrels who jump
from branch to branch
of the old black walnut tree.
But once,
someone lived here.
How can you tell?
Look. A chimney, made of stone,
back there, half-standing yet, though honeysuckle's
grown around it—there must
have been a house here. Look.
Push aside these weeds—here's
a stone foundation, laid on earth.
The house once here was built on it.
And if there was a house, there was
a family.
Dig in the dirt, scratch deep, and what
do you find?
A round blue glass marble, a nail.
A horseshoe and a piece
of plate. A small yellow bottle. A china doll's arm.

Listen. Can you listen, back, far back?
No, not the wind, that's now. But listen,
back, and hear:
a man's voice, scratchy-sweet, singing "Amazing Grace,"
a rocking chair squeaking, creaking on a porch,
the bubbling hot fat in a black skillet, the chicken frying,
and "Tommy! Get in here this minute! If I have to call you
one more time—!"
and "Ah, me, it's hot," and "Reckon it'll storm?"
"I don't know, I sure hope, we sure could use it,"
and "Supper! Supper tiiiiime!"
If you look, you can almost see them:
the boy at dusk, scratching in the dirt with his stick, the
uneven swing hanging vacant
in the black walnut tree, listless in the heat;
the girl, upstairs, combing out her long, long hair, unpinning,
unbraiding, and combing, by an oval mirror;
downstairs, Papa washing dishes as Mama sweeps the floor
and Uncle Ferd, Mama's brother, coming in, whistling, back
from shutting up the chickens
for the night, wiping the sweat
from his forehead.
"Ah, Lord, it's hot, even late as it is,"
"Yes, it surely is."
Someone swats
at a mosquito.
Bedtime.

But in that far-back summer night,
the swing begins to sway
as the wind comes up
as the rain comes down
there's thunder there's lightning (that's just like now)
the dry dusty earth soaks up the water
the roots of the plants, like the daffodil bulbs
the mama planted, hidden under the earth, but alive
and growing, the roots
drink it up. A small green snake
coils happily in the wet woods,
and Timmy sleeps straight through the storm. Anne, the girl, who
wishes for a yellow hair ribbon, wakes, and then returns to
sleep, like Uncle Ferd, sighing as he dreams
of walking down a long road with change in his pocket. But
the mother wakes, and wakes the father, her husband,
and they sit on the side of the bed,
and watch the rain together,
without saying a word, in the house where everyone else
still sleeps. Her head on Papa's shoulder,
her long hair falling down her back, she's wearing
a white nightgown
that makes her look
almost like a ghost when the lightning flashes.

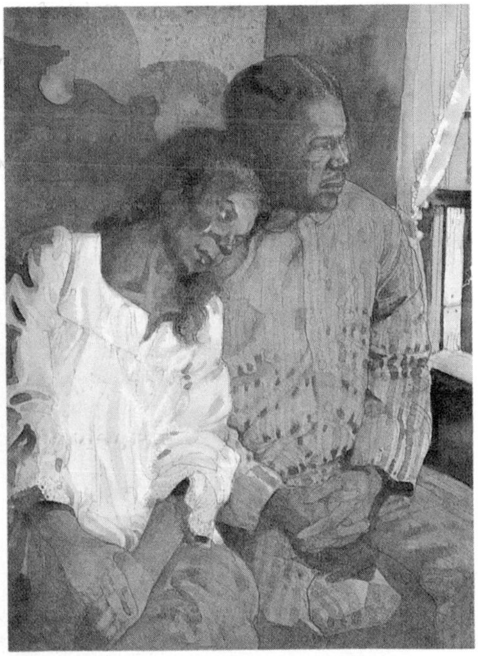

And now, she *is* a ghost, and we
can only see her
if we try. We're not sure
if we're making her up, or if
we really can see her, imagining
the home place as it might have been, or was, before
the house burned down, or everyone moved away
and the woods moved in.
Her son and daughter, grown and gone, her brother
who went to Chicago, her husband, even
her grandchildren, even her house,

all gone, almost as gone as if
they had never laughed and eaten chicken and rocked,
played and fought and made up,
combed hair and washed dishes and swept,
sang and scratched at mosquito bites.
Almost as gone, but
not quite. Not quite.
They were here.
This was their home.
For each year, in a quiet green place,
where there's only a honeysuckle-vined chimney
to tell you there was ever a house
(if, that is, you happen to travel that way,
and wonder, like we did);
where there's only a marble, a nail, a horseshoe, a piece
of plate, a piece of doll,
a single rotted almost-gone piece of rope swaying
on a black walnut tree limb,
to tell you there was ever a family here;
only deer and raccoons and squirrels
instead of people
to tell you there were living creatures;
each year, still,
whether anyone sees, or not,
whether anyone listens, or not,
the daffodils come up,
to trumpet their good news
forever and forever.

BIBLIOGRAPHY

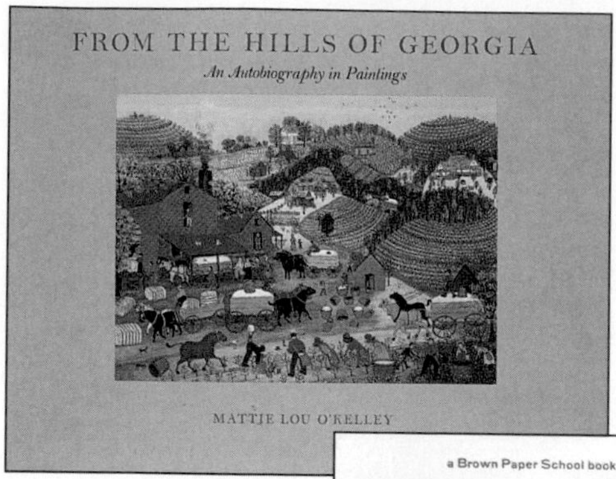

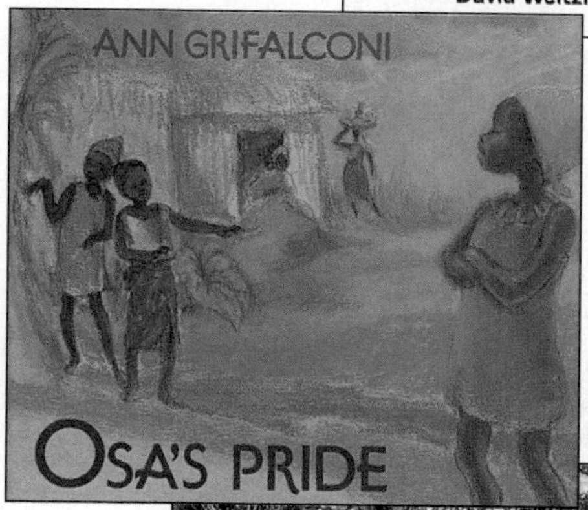

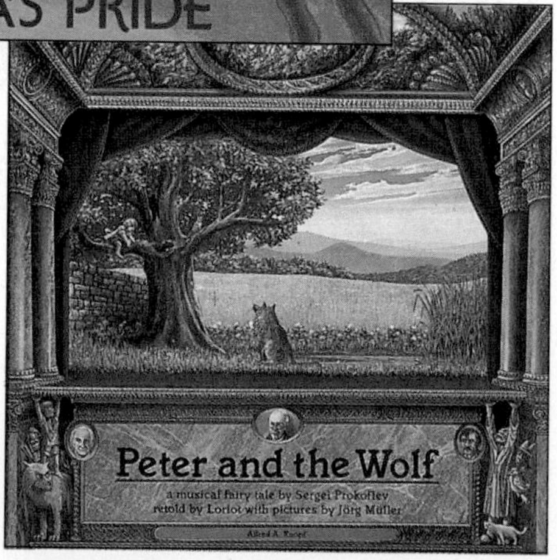

From the Hills of Georgia: An Autobiography in Paintings by Mattie Lou O'Kelley. Folk artist Mattie Lou O'Kelley has put together some of her "storytelling" paintings to make a visual autobiography. She has added some personal memories of her childhood.

My Backyard History Book by David Weitzman. Here's a collection of activities and projects that show how learning the story of your past begins at home. You might choose to make a time capsule, do a gravestone rubbing, or trace your genealogy.

Osa's Pride by Ann Grifalconi. Osa's grandmother uses a story cloth to tell a tale that helps Osa solve a problem she has.

Peter and the Wolf is a musical fairy tale composed by Sergei Prokofiev. This version is retold by Loriot, with pictures by Jörg Müller. It's a great example of a story told through music. The book is available with a narrated audiocassette with music performed by the Hamburg Symphony Orchestra.

The Talking Bird and the Story Pouch by Amy Lawson. Storyteller, whose calling as a storyteller has been passed down the generations, sets off on a magical adventure in search of stories. He soon discovers the storytelling powers within himself.

Tell Me a Story, Mama by Angela Johnson. A little girl remembers all the stories about her mama's childhood—almost better than her mama does.

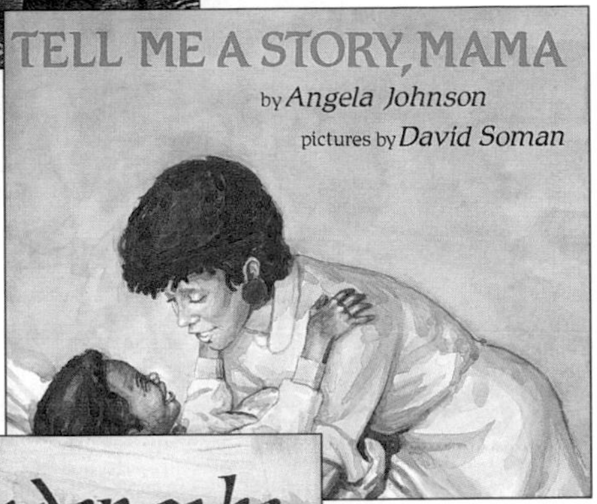

Thunder Cake by Patricia Polacco. What is a Thunder Cake? Find out how a little girl loses her fear of thunderstorms when her understanding grandmother tells her the story of the "Thunder Cake."

The Totem Pole Indians of the Northwest by Don E. Beyer. Interested in totem poles? This more detailed description will help you learn more about the totem pole Indians of the Pacific Northwest.

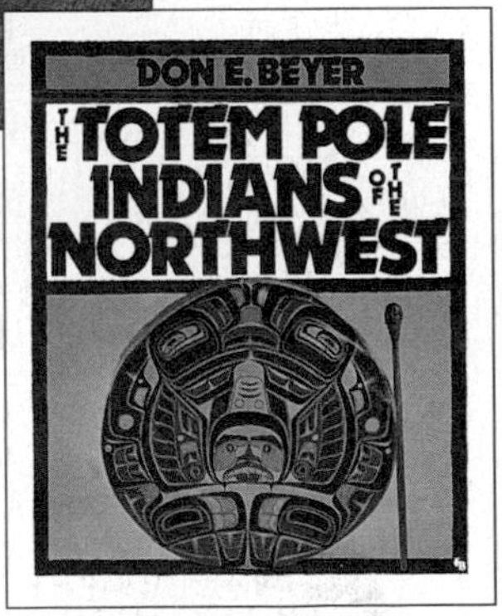

GLOSSARY

PRONUNCIATION KEY

a as in **a**t	**o** as in **o**x	**ou** as in **ou**t	**ch** as in **ch**air
ā as in l**a**te	**ō** as in r**o**se	**u** as in **u**p	**hw** as in **wh**ich
â as in c**a**re	**ô** as in b**ou**ght and r**aw**	**ûr** as in t**ur**n; g**er**m, l**ear**n, f**ir**m, w**or**k	**ng** as in ri**ng**
ä as in f**a**ther	**oi** as in c**oi**n	**ə** as in **a**bout, chick**e**n, penc**i**l, cann**o**n, circ**u**s	**sh** as in **sh**op
e as in s**e**t	**o͝o** as in b**oo**k		**th** as in **th**in
ē as in m**e**	**o͞o** as in t**oo**		**t͟h** as in **th**ere
i as in **i**t	**or** as in f**or**m		**zh** as in trea**s**ure
ī as in k**i**te			

The mark (ˊ) is placed after a syllable with a heavy accent, as in **chicken** (chikˊ ən).
The mark (ˊ) after a syllable shows a lighter accent, as in **disappear** (disˊ ə pērˊ).

abandon (ə banˊ dən) *v.* To leave empty.
absorb (ab sorbˊ) *v.* To soak up.
abundantly (ə bunˊ dənt lē) *adv.* With more than enough; richly; well.
ache (āk) *v.* To have pain.
acre (āˊ kər) *n.* An amount of land that is about one-third of a city block in size; 43,560 square feet.
adapt (ə daptˊ) *v.* To fit in.
adequate (adˊ i kwit) *adj.* As much as needed; enough.
adorn (ə dornˊ) *v.* To decorate.
adze (adz) *n.* A tool with a sharp blade for carving wood.
affectionate (ə fekˊ shə nit) *adj.* Friendly; loving.
affordable (ə forˊ də bəl) *adj.* Cheap enough to buy; not costing too much money for someone to buy.
ailanthus tree (ā lanˊ thəs trēˊ) *n.* A wide-spreading tree with long leaves and thick clusters of flowers.
allergic (ə lûrˊ jik) *adj.* Having an unpleasant reaction to certain things.
ambition (am bishˊ ən) *n.* A strong desire for success.
amidst (ə midstˊ) *prep.* In the middle of.

analyze (an′ l īz′) *v.* To examine the parts of something.

ancestor (an′ ses tər) *n.* A parent, grandparent, great-grandparent, and so on.

aphid (ā′ fid) *n.* A tiny insect that lives on the juice of plants.

arctic (ärk′ tik) *adj.* Having to do with the area around the North Pole.

aroma (ə rō′ mə) *n.* A good smell.

artificial (är′ tə fish′ əl) *adj.* Made by people rather than nature.

aspect (as′ pekt) *n.* Point of view; part.

asphalt (as′ fôlt) *n.* A substance that is like tar, used to pave streets.

atmosphere (at′ məs fēr′) *n.* The mood or feeling.

away (ə wā′) *v.* To go somewhere.

awning (ô′ ning) *n.* A canvas cover for a door or window to shade the sun.

babushka (bə b o͝osh′ kə) *n.* A head scarf shaped like a triangle.

bale (bāl) *n.* A large bundle of hay, packed tightly and tied together.

ballad (bal′ əd) *n.* A simple song or poem that tells a story.

banquet (bang′ kwit) *n.* A feast; a large dinner.

barter (bär′ tər) *v.* To trade things instead of using money.

beckon (bek′ ən) *v.* To invite someone by waving.

befriend (bi frend′) *v.* To help; to be a friend to.

bewilder (bi wil′ dər) *v.* To confuse; to puzzle.

biologist (bī ol′ ə jist) *n.* A person who studies plants and animals.

bobsled (bob′ sled′) *n.* A large sled that has a steering wheel and brakes.

boisterous (boi′ stər əs) *adj.* Noisy.

bolster (bōl′ stər) *v.* To support; to make stronger.

bosom (bo͝oz′ əm) *n.* The chest; the heart.

botherment (both′ ər mənt) *n.* A feeling of worry.

bounteous (boun′ tē əs) *adj.* Full; plentiful.

boutique (bo͞o tēk′) *n.* A small shop.

burdock (bûr′ dok) *n.* A weed with coarse, broad leaves and prickly heads or burs.

butternut (but′ ər nut′) *n.* The nut of a butternut tree, related to the walnut family.

cable car (kā′ bəl kär′) *n.* A vehicle that looks like a bus and is pulled by a thick bunch of wires.

Pronunciation Key: at; lāte; câre; fäther; set; mē; it; kīte; ox; rōse; ô in bought; coin; bo͝ok; to͞o; form; out; up; tûrn; ə sound in about, chicken, pencil, cannon, circus; chair; hw in which; ring; shop; thin; t̶here; zh in treasure.

calabash (kal′ ə bash′) *n.* The shell of a dried gourd, used as a bowl.

camouflage (kam′ ə fläzh′) *v.* To disguise; to hide.

caraway (kar′ ə wā′) *n.* A plant related to parsley.

cavity (kav′ i tē) *n.* A small hole; a hollow.

challah (hä′ lə) *n.* A bread, which is often braided, made with eggs. Challah is eaten on the Jewish Sabbath.

charred (chärd) *adj.* Burned-looking.

clamor (klam′ ər) *n.* A loud, lengthy noise.

clapper (klap′ ər) *n.* The part of a bell that strikes the sides and makes a noise.

clutch (kluch) *n.* A group of eggs to be hatched.

commute (kə myo͞ot′) *v.* To travel between two places every day.

complex (kom′ pleks) *n.* A group of related things.

compost heap (kom′ pōst hēp′) *n.* A stored mixture of rotting plants and food scraps to be used as fertilizer.

condescend (kon′ də send′) *v.* To act as if one is too good to do something.

content (kən tent′) *adj.* Satisfied; pleased.

converge (kən vûrj′) *v.* To come together from different places.

corkscrew (kork′ skro͞o′) *v.* To move by turning back and forth or twisting.

crackerjack (krak′ ər jak′) *adj.* Extremely good.

cranny (kran′ ē) *n.* A slit; a narrow opening.

creation (krē ā′ shən) *n.* Something that is made.

crevice (krev′ is) *n.* A crack.

crimson (krim′ zən) *adj.* Deep red.

crinkle (kring′ kəl) *v.* 1. To wrinkle. 2. To make tiny, sharp sounds.

culture (kul′ chər) *n.* The ways of living of a group of people, passed down from one generation to the next.

culvert (kul′ vərt) *n.* A large drain pipe that goes under a road.

curdle (kûr′ dl) *v. slang.* To feel sour or sad.

currant (kûr′ ənt) *n.* A small, seedless raisin.

curtsy (kûrt′ sē) *n.* A greeting in which women and girls bend the knees and lower the body.

dainty (dān′ tē) *n.* A special, delicious food.
debris (də brē′) *n.* Rubbish; trash.
debt (det) *n.* 1. Money that is owed. 2. The condition of owing money.
decade (dek′ ād) *n.* A period of ten years.
decompose (dē′ kəm pōz′) *v.* To rot.
dense (dens) *adj.* Thick.
depression (di presh′ ən) *n.* A shallow hole or a dent.
descendant (di sen′ dənt) *n.* A person's child or the child's child, and so on; anyone born from a particular family line.
deter (di tûr′) *v.* To hold back; to prevent.
dialect (dī′ ə lekt′) *n.* The version or form of a language spoken by a certain group of people.
dialogue (dī′ ə lôg′) *n.* Words spoken between two or more people in a story or book.
discard (di skärd′) *v.* To throw away.
dismay (dis mā′) *n.* A feeling of being discouraged.
dither (diŧħ′ ər) *n.* An upset, confused feeling.
divider (di vī′ dər) *n.* Anything that cuts a thing into parts.
dorsal (dor′ səl) *adj.* On the upper side of the body; on the back.
drought (drout) *n.* Dry weather that lasts a very long time.
dweller (dwel′ ər) *n.* Someone who lives in a certain place.
dwelling (dwel′ ing) *n.* A place to live.

ebb (eb) *v.* To flow away.
economics (ek′ ə nom′ iks) *n.* The study of money and costs.
elder (el′ dər) *n.* An official in certain churches.
elevated (el′ ə vā′ tid) *adj.* Raised up.
elevator (el′ ə vā′ tər) *n.* A building in which grain is handled and stored.
embroidery (em broi′ də rē) *n.* A design or picture sewn with needle and thread.
emigrate (em′ i grāt′) *v.* To leave a country in order to live in another country.
encounter (en koun′ tər) *v.* To meet by chance.
endure (en d o͞o r′) *v.* To put up with; to bear.
environment (en vī′ rən mənt) *n.* Everything surrounding a plant, animal, or person.
etch (ech) *v.* To outline clearly.
exaggerate (ig zaj′ ə rāt′) *v.* To say something is bigger or more important than it really is.

Pronunciation Key: at; lāte; câre; fäther; set; mē; it; kīte; ox; rōse; ô in bought; coin; bo͝ok; to͞o; form; out; up; tûrn; ə sound in about, chicken, pencil, cannon, circus; chair; hw in which; ring; shop; thin; t̶here; zh in treasure.

exhaust (ig zôst´) *n.* The gases and smoke from a car that go into the air.
exploration (ek´ splə rā´ shən) *n.* The act of searching or looking closely at a new area.

falcon (fôl´ kən) *n.* A powerful bird of prey.
fascinate (fas´ ə nāt´) *v.* To interest a great deal.
faze (fāz) *v.* To bother.
feat (fēt) *n.* A great act or deed.
feature (fē´ chər) *v.* To have in an important place.
fennel (fen´ l) *n.* A plant related to parsley.
fertile (fûr´ tl) *adj.* Fruitful; productive.
fertilizer (fûr´ tl ī´ zər) *n.* Material put into the soil to make it richer.
flamboyant (flam boi´ ənt) *adj.* Showy; bold; striking.
flax (flaks) *n.* A plant that is made into thread that is made into linen.
flimsy (flim´ zē) *adj.* Weak; slight; breakable.

florist (flor´ ist) *n.* A person who sells flowers.
flourish (flûr´ ish) *v.* To grow well; to succeed.
folklore (fōk´ lor´) *n.* The legends, beliefs, and customs of a people.
forsaken (for sā´ kən) *v.* A past tense of **forsake:** To abandon; to give up.
foundation (foun dā´ shən) *n.* The base of a house.
fragrant (frā´ grənt) *adj.* Sweet-smelling.
Frau (frou) *n.* The German title of address for a married woman, like *Mrs.*
frolic (frol´ ik) *n.* A party at which work is done.
frond (frond) *n.* A very large leaf.

generation (jen´ ə rā´ shən) *n.* A group of people who are about the same age.
genuine (jen´ yo͞o in) *adj.* Real.
gnarled (närld) *adj.* Full of twists and bumps; knotted.
gnawing (nô´ ing) *n.* A dull pain; the pain of hunger.
Gothic (goth´ ik) *adj.* A style of art that uses much detail and decoration.
gourd (gord) *n.* A melon-shaped fruit that can be dried, scooped out, and used as a bowl.
graze (grāz) *v.* To eat grass.

greenhouse (grēn´ hous´) *n.* A building for growing plants.
grieve (grēv) *v.* To make sad.
griot (grē ō´) *n.* A person in a tribe whose job is to remember the oral history of all the families in the tribe or village.

habitat (hab´ i tat´) *n.* The natural surroundings of a plant or animal.
haltingly (hôl´ ting lē) *adv.* In a slow way.
handcrafted (hand´ kraft´ əd) *adj.* Made by hand, not by machine.
hearty (här´ tē) *adj.* Big; filling.
heritage (her´ i tij) *n.* The things or ideas handed down from people who lived before.
hesitate (hez´ i tāt´) *v.* To pause; to be unsure.
hobble (hob´ əl) *v.* To limp.
homesite (hōm´ sīt´) *n.* The land for a house.
hover (huv´ ər) *v.* To hang in the air near something.
hue (hyo͞o) *n.* A shade of color.
huppa (ho͝o´ pə) *n.* A covering that stands like a tent above the bride and groom in a Jewish wedding.

idleness (īd´ l nis) *n.* A lack of activity; not working.
immature (im´ ə cho͝or´) *adj.* Not fully grown.
imprint (im´ print) *n.* A mark made by something pressing.
incite (in sīt´) *v.* To urge on; to stir up.
inherit (in her´ it) *v.* To receive another person's property after his or her death.
insert (in sûrt´) *v.* To put into.
inspire (in spīr´) *v.* To cause.
install (in stôl´) *v.* To place a thing where it is going to be used.
intersection (in´ tər sek´ shən) *n.* The place where two streets cross each other.
intruder (in tro͞o´ dər) *n.* Someone who enters a place against the owner's will.
island (ī´ lənd) *n.* 1. A piece of land surrounded by water. 2. Anything surrounded by something else.

jostle (jos´ əl) *v.* To bump into.

ladle (lād´ l) *n.* A long-handled cup for serving liquids.

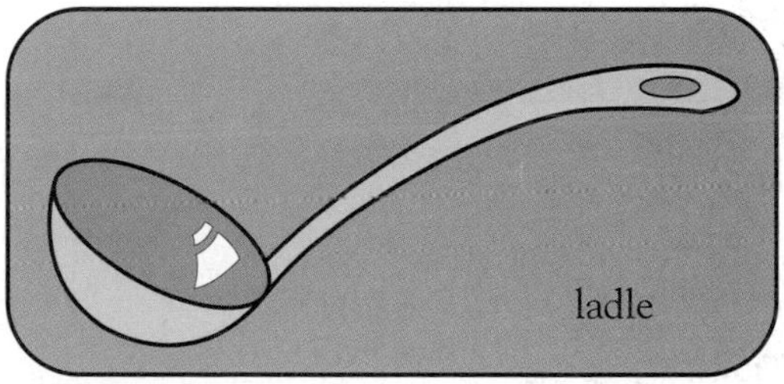

laprobe (lap´ rōb´) *n.* A blanket used outdoors.
latex gum (lā´ teks gum´) *n.* A sticky liquid taken from a plant.

Pronunciation Key: at; lāte; câre; fäther; set; mē; it; kīte; ox; rōse; ô in bought; coin; bo͝ok; to͞o; form; out; up; tûrn; ə sound in about, chicken, pencil, cannon, circus; chair; hw in which; ring; shop; thin; there; zh in treasure.

lease (lēs) *n.* An agreement to rent something.
lifespan (līf′ span′) *n.* The amount of time a thing lives.
limply (limp′ lē) *adv.* Loosely.
literature (lit′ ər ə chər) *n.* Books, poems, and plays that have value.
livelihood (līv′ lē ho͝od′) *n.* A way of making a living.
lovage (luv′ ij) *n.* A plant related to parsley.
lurch (lûrch) *n.* A sudden movement to the side.
lush (lush) *adj.* Fresh; tender; abundant.
luxury (luk′ shə rē) *n.* Anything a person cannot afford.

manufacturing (man′ yə fak′ chər ing) *n.* Making things by machine in a factory.
manuscript (man′ yə skript′) *n.* A book or paper written by hand.
mathematician (math′ ə mə tish′ ən) *n.* A person who works with numbers.
medieval (mē′ dē ē′ vəl) *adj.* Having to do with the Middle Ages in Europe (about A.D. 400–1400).
merge (mûrj) *v.* To be mixed together.
metallic (mə tal′ ik) *adj.* As if made by metal.
microscope (mī′ krə skōp′) *n.* An instrument that makes small things look larger.
migrate (mī′ grāt) *v.* To move from colder to warmer lands and back again.
migratory (mī′ grə tor′ ē) *adj.* Moving one's home with the seasons.
miniature (min′ ē ə chər) *adj.* Tiny; very small.
mode (mōd) *n.* A way.
molt (mōlt) *v.* To drop off feathers.
morsel (mor′ səl) *n.* A small piece of food.
mortar (mor′ tər) *n.* A mixture like cement used to hold bricks together.
mortgage (mor′ gij) *n.* The money borrowed to buy a house.
mottled (mot′ ld) *adj.* Spotted or blotched with different colors.
mound (mound) *n.* A pile or heap of something.
musty (mus′ tē) *adj.* Stale; moldy.
myth (mith) *n.* A story or legend from olden days that tries to explain something.

nanny (nan´ ē) *n.* A person hired to live in the home and care for a child.
nestling (nest´ ling) *n.* A bird too young to leave the nest.
newsstand (no͞oz´ stand´) *n.* An outdoor booth where newspapers are sold.
nonstop (non´ stop´) *adv.* Constantly; all the time.
nook (no͝ok) *n.* A small, hidden place.
nursery (nûr´ sə rē) *n.* A place where plants are raised.

obedience (ō bē´ dē əns) *n.* Following the rules.
observant (əb zûr´ vənt) *adj.* Watchful; careful.
observe (əb zûrv´) *v.* To see; to look at.
occupation (ok´ yə pā´ shən) *n.* A type of job.
oral (or´ əl) *adj.* Spoken.
Ordnung (ord´ nəng) *n.* The Amish laws.
organdy (or´ gən dē) *n.* A smooth, stiff cotton material.
organic (or gan´ ik) *adj.* Produced by living things.
original (ə rij´ ə nl) *adj.* First.
originally (ə rij´ ə nl ē) *adv.* At first; in the beginning.
outwit (out´ wit´) *v.* To beat by being sly.
oval (ō´ vəl) *adj.* Egg-shaped.
overpass (ō´ vər pas´) *n.* A road that crosses above another road.

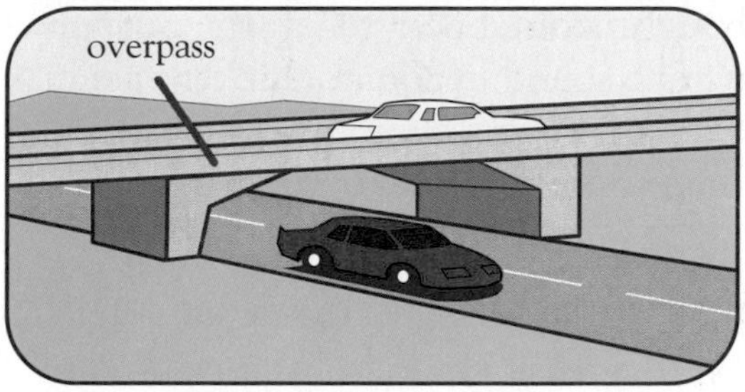

parachute (par´ ə sho͞ot´) *n.* An umbrella-shaped object that helps other objects float down slowly from heights.
parasite (par´ ə sīt´) *n.* An animal that lives and feeds on another animal.
partial (pär´ shəl) *adj.* Not complete.
particular (pər tik´ yə lər) *adj.* Only; special.
passageway (pas´ ij wā´) *n.* A narrow place to walk between two buildings.
patriotic (pā´ trē ot´ ik) *adj.* Loyal to one's country.
penetrate (pen´ i trāt´) *v.* To break through; to cut into.
pennyroyal (pen´ ē roi´ əl) *n.* A plant related to mint.
peregrine (per´i grin) *n.* A type of falcon that catches other birds in flight.
persecution (pûr´ si kyo͞o´ shən) *n.* Bad treatment.
persnickety (pər snik´ i tē) *adj.* Very fussy; careful.

Pronunciation Key: at; lāte; câre; fäther; set; mē; it; kīte; ox; rōse; ô in bought; coin; bo͝ok; to͞o; form; out; up; tûrn; ə sound in about, chicken, pencil, cannon, circus; chair; hw in which; ring; shop; thin; t̶here; zh in treasure.

petroleum jelly (pe´ trō′ lē əm jel′ ē) *n.* A greasy, sticky substance used to coat things.
pitifully (pit′ i flē) *adv.* Sadly.
plantain (plan′ tin) *n.* A weed that has large leaves and long spikes with small flowers.
plaster (plas′ tər) *n.* A substance like cement that is used to make walls and ceilings.
pleasure (plezh′ ər) *v.* To please; to satisfy.
political (pə lit′ i kəl) *adj.* Having to do with the government of a country.
pollution (pə lo͞o′ shən) *n.* Harmful or dirty material added to the air, water, or soil.
portion (por′ shən) *n.* A part.
poverty (pov′ ər tē) *n.* The state of being poor.
preserve (pri zûrv′) *v.* To keep safe.
prickly (prik′ lē) *adj.* Full of sharp points that stick or sting.
profitable (prof′ i tə bəl) *adj.* Making money; gainful.
propose (prə pōz′) *v.* To offer a plan; to suggest.
questioningly (kwes′ chən ing lē) *adv.* In a wondering way.
quote (kwōt) *v.* To state a price for something.

rabies (rā′ bēz) *n.* A disease spread by animal bites. Rabies usually causes death unless treated.
rampage (ram′ pāj) *v.* To act wild.
realty (rē′ əl tē) *n.* Property, including land and buildings; real estate.
reaper (rē′ pər) *n.* A farm machine for cutting grain in the fields.
recite (ri sīt′) *v.* To tell aloud.
recollection (rek´ ə lek′ shən) *n.* A story remembered.
record (rek′ ərd) *n.* A piece of writing that tells a memory of some facts or events. —*v.* (ri kord′) To write down facts or information about events.
regard (ri gärd′) *v.* To consider.
reign (rān) *v.* To rule.
reject (ri jekt′) *v.* To refuse; to cast away.
reluctantly (ri luk′ tənt lē) *adv.* Not willingly.
replenish (ri plen′ ish) *v.* To fill up again.
research (ri sûrch′) *v.* To seek new knowledge.
reserve (ri zûrv′) *v.* To set aside for later use.
responsibility (ri spon´ sə bil′ i tē) *n.* A duty; a job.

retire (ri tīr′) *v.* To stop working for the rest of one's life.
revolt (ri vōlt′) *v.* To rebel; to rise against or overthrow a ruler.
rickety (rik′ i tē) *adj.* Shaky; wobbly.
rodent (rōd′ nt) *n.* A type of animal that gnaws with big front teeth. Rodents include mice, rats, beavers, squirrels, and chipmunks.
rosemary (rōz′ mâr′ ē) *n.* A plant related to mint.
rotation (rō tā′ shən) *n.* Taking turns planting different crops in different years on the same land.
routine (ro͞o tēn′) *n.* The same actions done over and over.
rubble (rub′ əl) *n.* Rough, broken brick or stone.
rue (ro͞o) *n.* A strong-smelling plant with yellow flowers and leaves.
rural (ro͝or′ əl) *adj.* In the country.

sage (sāj) *n.* A plant related to mint.
savory (sā′ və rē) *n.* A plant related to mint.
scaffold (skaf′ əld) *n.* A framework that holds up something.
seasonal (sē′ zə nl) *adj.* Ripe at a certain time of the year.
security (si kyo͝or′ i tē) *n.* Safety.
seedling (sēd′ ling) *n.* A very young plant.
seldom (sel′ dəm) *adv.* Rarely; not often.
self-sufficient (self′ sə fish′ ənt) *adj.* Able to live on one's own; able to supply all one's own food, shelter, clothing, and other needs.
sensitive (sen′ si tiv) *adj.* 1. Easily affected; easily hurt. 2. Able to feel things well.
sewer (so͞o′ ər) *n.* An underground pipe that carries dirty water away from buildings.
shades (shādz) *n.* Sunglasses.
shawl (shôl) *n.* A covering for the head and shoulders.
shingle (shing′ gəl) *n.* A thin piece of wood used to cover roofs.

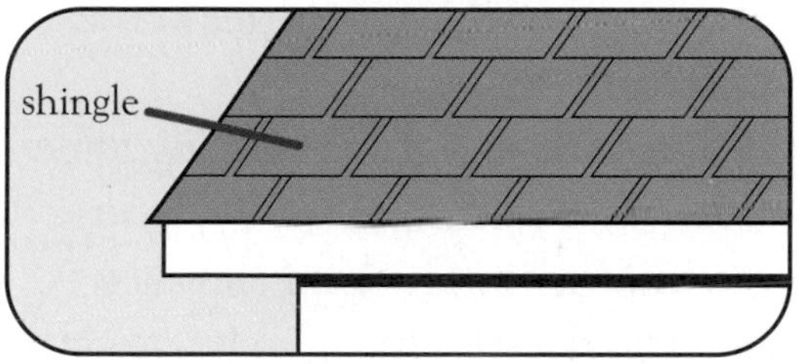

shrivel (shriv′ əl) *v.* To wrinkle and become smaller; to dry up and waste away.
shun (shun) *v.* To keep away from.
silo (sī′ lō) *n.* A tall building for storing food for animals on a farm.
simplicity (sim plis′ i tē) *n.* The state of being sincere, honest, natural, or plain.
soar (sor) *v.* To fly at a great height.
species (spē′ shēz) *n.* An animal family; a kind of animal.
sprawl (sprôl) *v.* To spread out.

Pronunciation Key: at; lāte; câre; fäther; set; mē; it; kīte; ox; rōse; ô in bought; coin; bo͝ok; to͞o; form; out; up; tûrn; ə sound in about, chicken, pencil, cannon, circus; chair; hw in which; ring; shop; thin; t͟here; zh in treasure.

squash (skwosh) *v.* To crush; to squeeze flat.

stalk (stôk) *n.* The stem of a plant.

staple (stā′ pəl) *n.* A basic food; a food used often.

stout (stout) *adj.* Sturdy; strong.

strewn (stro͞on) *v.* A past tense of **strew:** To scatter; to spread around.

suburb (sub′ ûrb) *n.* A town on the outer edge of a larger city.

suction (suk′ shən) *n.* A pulling force that uses a sucking action.

suet (so͞o′ it) *n.* The hard fat taken from cattle and sheep.

surge (sûrj) *v.* To swell; to heave; to move like a wave.

surplus (sûr′ plus) *n.* An amount more than is needed; an extra amount.

survival (sər vī′ vəl) *n.* The act of living; staying alive.

swerve (swûrv) *v.* To turn to one side suddenly.

sycamore (sik′ ə mor′) *n.* A shade tree; a buttonwood tree.

tamp (tamp) *v.* To force something to lay flat by hitting it.

tatter (tat′ ər) *v.* To tear.

teeming (tē′ ming) *adj.* Swarming; filled with.

temperature (tem′ pər ə chər) *n.* The hotness or coldness of a thing.

tempting (temp′ ting) *adj.* Attractive; desirable.

terrapin (ter′ ə pin) *n.* A type of turtle.

theoretically (thē′ ə ret′ i klē) *adv.* According to ideas; supposedly; in the mind.

thermos (thûr′ məs) *n.* A bottle for keeping liquids hot.

thrash (thrash) *v.* To beat.

thrive (thrīv) *v.* To survive; to do well.

thyme (tīm) *n.* A plant related to mint.

tinker (ting′ kər) *v.* To repair in a clumsy or makeshift way; to putter.

titmouse (tit′ mous′) *n.* A small, stout-billed songbird.

toil (toil) *v.* To work hard.

topmost (top′ mōst′) *adj.* Top; highest.

torrent (tor′ ənt) *n.* A swiftly rushing stream of water.

tradition (trə dish′ ən) *n.* A custom handed down through many generations.

tranquil (trang′ kwil) *adj.* Peaceful; calm.

translate (trans lāt′) *v.* To turn from one language into another.

transport (trans port´) *v.* To move goods from one place to another.

trestle (tres´ əl) *n.* A framework that holds up train tracks above a river or above the ground.

trillion (tril´ yən) *n.* The number 1,000,000,000,000; a very large number.

trudge (truj) *v.* To walk heavily and slowly.

tucker (tuk´ ər) *v.* To tire.

tundra (tun´ drə) *n.* In the arctic regions, a flat plain with no trees.

typical (tip´ i kəl) *adj.* Usual.

udder (ud´ ər) *n.* The part of a cow's body from which it gives milk.

unharness (un här´ nis) *v.* To take off the leather straps that fasten a horse to a buggy.

unpredictable (un´ pri dik´ tə bəl) *adj.* Not able to be planned; not certain.

untamed (un tāmd´) *adj.* Wild; in its natural state.

uppermost (up´ ər mōst´) *adj.* Highest.

urban (ûr´ bən) *adj.* In a city.

vacant (vā´ kənt) *adj.* Empty.

ventilation (ven´ tl ā´ shən) *n.* The process of bringing in fresh air.

visible (viz´ ə bəl) *adj.* Able to be seen.

vital (vīt´ l) *adj.* 1. Necessary. 2. Very important.

waft (wäft) *v.* To float on the air.

wharves (hworvz) *n.* Plural of **wharf:** A pier at which ships stop.

whittle (hwit´ l) *v.* To cut away pieces of wood with a knife.

wholesaler (hōl´ sāl´ ər) *n.* A business that sells to stores.

wilt (wilt) *v.* To droop; to fade.

windswept (wind´ swept´) *adj.* Blown by wind constantly.

woodland (wo͝od´ lənd) *adj.* From the woods or forests.

wormwood (wûrm´ wo͝od´) *n.* A shrub used in cooking and in medicine; sometimes called *sagebrush.*

worthwhile (wûrth´ hwīl´) *adj.* Important enough to do; rewarding.

yam (yam) *n.* A type of sweet potato.

yoke (yōk) *n.* A curved piece of wood that fits over an ox's neck. A yoke connects the ox to a cart.

zoologist (zō ol´ ə jist) *n.* A person who studies animals.

continued from page 5

Photography
157 Elaine S. Martens
167 Gretchen Tatge
247 AP/Wide World

COLOPHON

This book has been designed in the classic style to emphasize our commitment to classic literature. The typeface, Goudy Old Style, was drawn in 1915 by Frederic W. Goudy, who based it on fifteenth-century Italian letterforms.

The art has been drawn to reflect the golden age of children's book illustration and its recent rebirth in the work of innovative artists of today. This book was designed by John Grandits. Composition, electronic page makeup, and photo and art management were provided by The Chestnut House Group, Inc.